China Anthology

Seventy Years of Shanghai *Tiffin* Perspectives

Edited By

Victor T.H. Tsuan

and

Charles C. M. Chung

CHINA ANTHOLOGY

Seventy Years of Shanghai *Tiffin* Perspectives

Edited by:

Victor T.H. Tsuan,
&
Charles C.M. Chung

Cover design, illustrations & layout
by
Robert E. Whittaker

Published by **COMPASS** BOOKS - video - *films*
921 Jackson Drive
Cleveland WI, 53015
(414) 693-3345

Library of Congress Catalog Card Number: **96-84511**

International Standard Book Numbering (ISBN): 0-9639310-2-4

First Edition
1996

Printed in the United States of America

In commemorating the 70th anniversary of

the SHANGHAI *TIFFIN* CLUB of NEW YORK, Inc.

UNFORGETTABLE OLD FRIENDSHIP

by

Li-Fu Chen, LL.D.

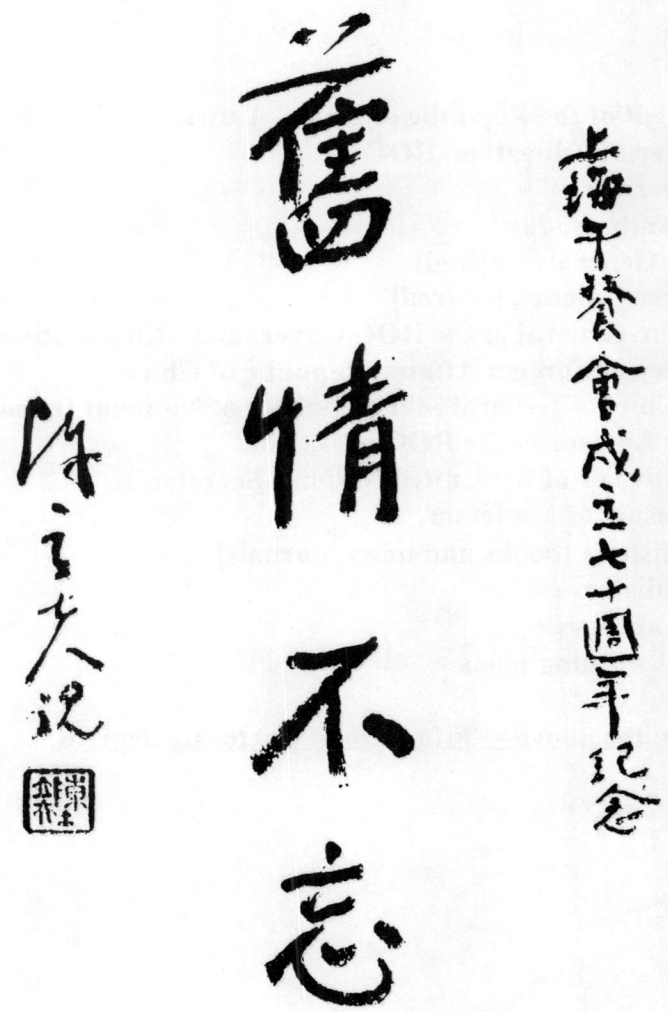

As publisher, it has been an honor to produce this important compilation of essays and memoirs so aptly chosen and edited by Dr. Victor T.H. Tsuan and Charles C.M. Chung for the **70th Anniversary of the Shanghai *Tiffin* Club of New York, Inc.**

Robert E. Whittaker

The thirty contributors of this anthology on CHINA consist of the following distinguished personages:

> **The President of the Republic of China, Taiwan**
> **The Minister of Education, ROC**
> **A U.S. Governor**
> **A former Ambassador**
> **Two Army Generals [retired]**
> **An Air Force Colonel, [retired]**
> **The Director-General of the ROC Government Information Office**
> **The Minister of Foreign Affairs, Republic of China**
> **A former Chief of General Staff, Minister of National Defense, ROC Premier and Senior Advisor to the ROC president.**
> **A former advisor of the United Nation's Secretariat**
> **Nine professors of academia**
> **Three publishers [books and news journals]**
> **Five journalists**
> **Four book authors**
> **Two award winning poets**
>
> **And among the above----Fifteen hold Doctorate degrees.**

This book is dedicated to the memory of:
The past presidents of the Shanghai *Tiffin* Club of New York

Dr. Bettis A. Garside
(12th President, 1943)

Edward G. Whittaker
(25th President, 1963-64)

1894 - 1989

1889 - 1978

Dr. Marguerite Daisy Atterbury (28th President, 1968)

1894 -1988

v

CONTENTS

+++++

PREFACE

An excellent summation as to the founding of the **Shanghai *Tiffin* Club of New York, Inc.,** is most ably stated in the Foreword of this publication.

How is it that such an organization has held together these seventy-two years? Certainly, those Americans abroad in the International Quarter of old Shanghai, formed rewarding friendships with the Chinese with whom they mixed socially and in business. They enjoyed a good and fascinating life. Trade flourished and the American dollar afforded them the best.

One thing - the Chinese definitely knew how to eat for both pleasure and health. Dining was never a "Fast Food" event. Today, the Westernization of Beijing and Shanghai are seen by the towering golden arches of McDonald's. Probably the old, relaxed approach to nourishment had more to do than anything with the longevity of our Club's "Old China Hands." This carried many of our members well into their nineties. For who could ask for better enjoyment than a sumptuous mid-day *"tiffin"* with a variety of Oriental dishes as a stimulant for vivid recollections of cherished Far Eastern memories.

Of course, those yesteryears were not all rickshaw rides to choice spots for refreshing repasts. Along with the activity in trade and missionary work, they kept trim by walking and cycling. There were some in the volunteer cavalry troop who not only patrolled the International Quarter, but also played polo against a team from Nanking. There were field sports which, in this case, included pole vaulting. There was also the North China tennis championship. The magnetic charm of old Shanghai was so strong for those absent for a time during World War II, that some braved the "Hump" as the only way back. The pull was so strong that one missionary and his two companions in a small boat under sail avoided the raging war in the Pacific to return via the Atlantic, rounding the Cape of Good Hope, then crossing the Indian Ocean, to find haven in that magnificent port.

With the passage of time, as "the days dwindle down to a precious few", a select number of the venerable "Old China Hands" concluded that they should meet to put together a permanent record of the best of the past and present from personal observations, stories and Club "tiffin" talks. This meeting convened in 1984 in a second floor balcony conference room of the Roosevelt Hotel in New York City.

One of the participants was a past re-elected Club President, a Chinese academic scholar and university professor. His recollections rounded out those of the other members. He was then, as now, Chairman of the Publications Committee and Executive Editor. He raised the funds necessary to enable a company in Chicago to provide two printings, thus meeting the demands for both paperback and hard cover.

The title for the first anthology he discovered in the Library of Congress: **For World Peace, Freedom and Justice Sixty Years: Shanghai *Tiffin* Perspective".** The hopeful aspect and reflection of events in the past many years made it seem definitely appropriate. For the last twenty-four years a safe buffer remained with China maintaining troops on its common border with Russia. Yet within the last decade in Europe, surprisingly, the Berlin Wall fell, the Soviet union dissolved, the Communist Block disappeared and an American President reactivated a 35 nation conference for joint confidence and security at the request of Russia to insure that a ban on chemical weapons would be agreed to and signed by all.

Ten years have now past and more since that earlier publication. Determined to out-do that first great effort, our senior Club Advisor and Chairman of the Publication Committee has assembled more anecdotes, Club talks, manuscripts of the past and present, plus updated views and writings of friends and members. This edition he named **CHINA *Anthology;* Seventy Years of Shanghai *Tiffin* Perspectives.** With the help of his generous committee, not only have sufficient funds been raised, but in addition, they have been able to arrange for the printing to be done at cost through the good offices of the son of another of our Club's Past Presidents.

With the sea of change in governments and alliances, we are well into a new world that can, if we all work together, bring many blessings. Throughout this change it behooves us all to remember the lessons of the past and incorporate them into the world of the next century. The stories, first hand accounts and anecdotes contained in the two anthologies can serve to help us remember these lessons as we move into the future.

What lies in store for us in the new millennium, we might ask? Our illustrious Editor has stated that he has every intention to publish his third anthology in the year 2004 A.D. Remember our "Old China Hands" and what they considered the secret of their longevity. Therefore, we should look forward to renewing our good Club friendships at our Chinese *tiffins* so that when the time comes, we may add the third Anthology to our bookshelves and also to the archives of the Library of Congress.

James Drummond Erskine, Lt. Colonel USAR-Ret.
   President of the **Shanghai *Tiffin* Club.**

Recipient of the following awards:

   The Order of the White Cloud
   The Chinese/American Academic and Professional Association Award
   Shanghai Tiffin Distinguished Service Award
   The Chinese Cultural Institute Award

++++++++

FOREWORD

The Shanghai Tiffin Club of New York was founded in 1924 by a group of Americans who had lived and worked in China, which consisted of Glenn Armstrong, Otto Metz, Ralph Sams, William J. Bray, Eugene T. McQuade and William Golding, who met for lunch on Monday, March 3, 1924 at *Ye Olde Dutch Tavern*, 15 John Street, Manhattan, New York.

In the course of the conversation, they found that many mutual friends from Shanghai were in New York City and that many changes had taken place among those they had known in China. Thus, they thought it would be a good idea to have a clearing house where names and addresses of former residents of China, their comings and goings, might be available to those in or near New York City. It gradually developed into a forum for the exchange of ideas on conditions in China and for the dissemination of knowledge about that country, in order to promote better understanding between the American and Chinese people. It believes that such understanding is conducive to world peace and may also help the cause of freedom, democracy and human rights.

On May 23, 1930, the Shanghai Tiffin Club of New York was duly incorporated under the Membership Corporation Law of the State of New York. It is listed as a non-profit organization with the identification number 23-7415-788, which entitles it to tax exemption in any business dealings. A copy of Certificate of Incorporation of our club has been kept on file at Lews, Garvin and Kelsey, a professional corporation of counselors at law, 120 Broadway, New York City, New York. Also the Bowery Bank has records of its dealings with our club.

Few Americans have had the intimate experience of actually having lived and worked among the Chinese people through those turbulent years of rapid and spectacular change, as have many of the members of our club. A few of the charter members are still living. They witnessed the overthrow of the Ch'ing Dynasty on October 10, 1911 and the establishment of the Government of **REPUBLIC of CHINA** on January 1, 1912. More recent members can recount their experience as prisoners of war of the Japanese and later of the Chinese Communists. They are known as "Old China Hands." Many of our members were in World War II and the United States Fourteenth Air Force, the renowned "Flying Tigers." Our membership also has some expatriated mainland Chinese and free Chinese from Taiwan. They have developed insights into the thoughts and feelings of the Chinese people and their civilization as well as way of life, which, needless to say are alien to our own in these United States of America. It is indeed a privilege to be associated with such a group of thoughtful and devoted members as we now have in our club.

The publication of this volume is in celebration of our club's seventieth anniversary. It was long overdue because of tardy fund raising efforts. All essays in this anthology have been contributed by members and friends of our club.

Acknowledgments are made of this generous help received throughout the long process of bringing this anthology into being. The Publication Committee has made no substantive changes in all the work in this volume. The responsibility for the contents of the essays rests with the authors as do copyrights to their own work.

The members of the Publication Committee wish to dedicate this book to the memory of our three distinguished past presidents: **Dr. Bettis A. Garside,** the twelfth president; **Mr. Edward G. Whittaker,** the twenty-fifth president; and **Dr. Marguerite Daisy Atterbury,** the twenty-eighth president. Their outstanding contributions and lofty purpose remain as a source of inspiration to the membership of our organization. Since a number of our members are also members of the World League for Freedom and Democracy, and it was the first time its annual conference was held in New York City in conjunction with the fiftieth anniversary celebration of the founding of the United Nations, the members of our publication committee also wish to dedicate this book to the twenty-seventh annual conference of the **World League for Freedom and Democracy.**

Finally, the publication committee acknowledges special indebtedness to the generous financial support of the Honorable **Li-Fu Chen,** Senior Adviser to the President; Mr. **Tih-Wu Wang,** President of the United Daily News, whose sudden passing makes us feel extremely sad, because his ardent wish to see the publication of this book was not fulfilled; **H.E. Ambassador Tzu-Dan Wu;** Mr. **Charles C. M. Chung,** co-editor of this anthology; Dr. **Diana L. Kao,** Professor Emeritus of City College of New York; Mr. **San-Yan Wong,** President of San Kiang Charitable Association Inc., and Miss **June L. Aulick,** a free-lance writer based in New York. Thanks are also due to Mrs. **Judy Atterbury Jenney,** Professor **Betty Lee Sung,** Miss **Elinor P. Griest,** Professor **Paul Hilaire,** Mr. **David A. Heinlein** and Mr. **Joseph R. Brown** for editing part of the manuscript.

I am particularly grateful to the co-editor of this volume, my friend Mr. **Charles C. M. Chung,** a leading scholar of the United Nations, who has contributed to this work in countless ways and from whose comments I have benefited at various stages. I wish also to thank our club's current President, Col. **James Drummond Erskine,** for his encouragement and editorial advice. Above all, this book could not have been completed without the tremendous assistance and support I was privileged to receive from my editor and publisher, Mr. **Robert E. Whittaker,** President / CEO of **COMPASS Books -** video-*films,* who in conversation and correspondence, has given his most generous help in ideas, time and effort, and making numerous valuable suggestions on substance, format and style, in addition to his kind offer to publish this book at cost. On behalf of the publication committee, I shall be forever grateful to him. To all of those mentioned and others who were not, we extend our deep appreciation.

March 12, 1996

Victor T. H. Tsuan, Ph.D., F.R.S.
Chairman; Publication Committee
Past President and Senior Adviser
Shanghai *Tiffin* Club of New York, Inc.

Chapter I

INFLUENTIAL POLITICAL LEADERS

GEORGE C. MARSHALL and I

by Li-fu Chen, LL.D.

On August 10th, 1945, Japan surrendered unconditionally. One day in November, Gimo Chiang invited me to lunch at his Wangshan residence. Chingkuo was also there. After lunch, ;Minister Wang Shi-chieh of Foreign Affairs came in with important matters, reporting that the United States Government decided to send General George C. Marshall to come to China to mediate the KMT-CCP dispute. After listening to the report, I quickly interjected by saying: "This is not going to work out. Anyone would be better than General Marshall himself." The Gimo questioned: "Why is that?"

I replied: "The KMT-CCP question would be much easier to resolve if the Soviet Union could be directly consulted. First, if the United States mediates, the Soviet Union would be offended, and the issue would become complicated. Secondly, the Communist side would, as I see it, be given advantage to procrastinate so as to gain more time to re-equip and regroup to fight against us. The united States which was not conversant with the CCP, would be susceptible to the communist deception: Finally the KMT-CCP disputes will have, according to my own estimation, little chance to succeed.

General Marshall, a world hero, assumed the role of being a mediator, who simply turned around and asked Minister Wang: "Has the cable of our concurrence gone:" "Yes, it has," Wang continued, "The Americans who know little about the Chinese Communists, may gain more understanding about them through their participation in the mediation effort." Gimo Chiang remained in a long period of silence. "Then, it will be too late to regret, if the future mediation effort fails to live up to its expectation," I added.

On December 22, 1945, General Marshall came to China as President Truman's special envoy to mediate the CCP-KMT dispute. December 24 was the General's birthday. The Gimo held a grand banquet reception in Marshall's honor to welcome him, as well as to celebrate his birthday. To everyone's surprise, General Marshall bitterly lectured us for doing this in such a haughty manner of a governor-general. All those government officials who attended the reception banquet, were quite upset. After the dinner, Gimo Chiang invited the four of us, General Marshall, Wang Chung-hui (Secretary-General of the KMT Central Committee) and myself, to gather around at one section of the room for an informal talk. At outset, the Gimo introduced General Marshall to each one of us and suggested to the General; "These three gentlemen will be at your disposal for consultation, should you want to know about the information concerning our party and government." The General had, subsequently, a brief exchange of remarks with three of us and then left.

The next day, Wang, Wu, and I paid a courtesy call on Marshall, repeatedly assuring him that if he needed any help, he should feel free to call on the three of us and we would do our best to cooperate with him. Never-the-less, after this meeting, we had never received any phone calls or messages from the General for consultation. A few weeks later, I discussed with Secretary-General Wu Tieh-ch'eng about whether the three of us should make another call on general Marshall. Wu took up the matter with Minister Wang Shi-chieh of Foreign Affairs, but Wang disapproved of it so the matter was dropped. A short time later, I was directed (by the government) to go to Shanghai to handle the local disturbance there. Leighton Stuart who was coincidentally passing through Shanghai on his way to Nanking, told me that General Marshall had sent for him by cable. Mr. Fu Ching-po (Leighton Stuart's aid) knew that I was in Shanghai at the time. Pan Kung-chan made an arrangement for me through Fu to meet with Leighton Stuart. As a result, we held a seven-hour lengthy discussion. As a matter of fact, during the war period, Mr. Leighton Stuart came to Chungking from time to time, and we were in constant contact with each other. I had often asked him to carry secret messages and relate them to the local school officials in Peiping on educational matters.

In meeting with him this time in Shanghai, I knew that Marshall's cable would certainly mean to offer him some important assignment. At this time quite a few left wing students of Yenking university had already infiltrated the American Embassy. In case that Leighton Stuart was appointed Ambassador, those left wing students would surely take full advantage of the opportunity to advance their cause. Subsequently, I used the occasion to advise Leighton Stuart in detail about the history of the KMT-CCP coalition so as to warn him to be vigilant of the communist plot against the government.

Leighton Stuart was a sincere and honest educator who had devoted himself to education for years. He was quite shocked to learn of the CCP plot. I felt that the seven-hour conversation between us would prove to be very helpful to Leighton Stuart in his later dealings with complex situations. Towards the end of our conversation, I suggested to him that he could intimate to General Marshall to get prepared in advance. Being on the government side, we wanted very much to exert our best effort to help the General fulfill his mission, but the Communist side merely traded negotiations for gaining more time with no purpose of achieving any results. Based on this rationale, what the General had hoped for would have had little chance to succeed. Thus, the general should be prepared for the worst.

On July 9, 1946, Leighton Stuart was appointed American Ambassador to China and presented his credentials on July 19. Sure enough, he told Marshall all that I had told him, and Marshall suspected that I had been prompted by Chiang. Actually, Chiang had never discussed Marshall with me. Long before Marshall came to China, I had expressed by views to Chiang. events only proved my predictions were correct.

One day, General Marshall met with Generalissimo Chiang and said: "Ambassador Leighton Stuart met with Chen Li-fu in shanghai and Chen told him that my mission is bound to fail and that I should be prepared for that." Then he asked, "is it true or not?" The Gimo replied with a smile: "Chen Li-fu went to Shanghai for official business. I have not seen him for several weeks. Chen is a thoughtful man of philosophy, why have you not invited him for a talk?" Later, the General was looking every where for me in hope of having a talk with me. Afterwards I received a long distance call from my family about it and rushed back to Nanking from Shanghai. I went to General Marshall's residence for the appointment at 4:15 p.m.

At first, Marshall did not seem very friendly when he asked me about my attitude toward the peace talks between the Kuomintang and the Communists. I said: "I am a member of the Kuomingtang, moreover the director of it's Organization Department. At these meetings we are free to speak out, whether pro or con, about the peace talks. But once the Kuomintang has made its decision, every party member must obey. As the director of the Organization Department I particularly should set an example."

Marshall said: "Chou En-lai says you are sabotaging the peace talks, you are against me, and you personally directed your people to attack their *New China Daily [Hsin-hua jih-pao]* office at Chiao-Ch'ang-Kou in Chungking. Is that true?"

I asked, "Do you have an concrete evidence?" I told him that as a student of mining engineering I respected science and was ashamed of such absurd nonsense. I assured him that Chou's words were sheer smear, and I added: "I remember that day you first arrived in China when, after the banquet, the Generalissimo had specifically introduced Wang Ch'ung-hui, We T'ieh-ch'eng and myself to consult with you. We even called on you the next day, repeating our offer of service. But months passed and you never contacted us. I first thought that you must already be very knowledgeable about Kuomingtang affairs. After listening to you, I realize that what you know are the statements of only one of the parties, which contrast sharply with facts. No wonder the peace negotiation is having difficulties. If you have the time, I am willing to tell how it happened."

Marshall said, "Please go on."

Thereupon I stated that, after eight years of war, we welcomed peace negotiations so that the National Government would have a chance to catch its breath, to rebuild it's army, and to reconstruct the country. Who would not have embraced such an opportunity? Moreover, the Kuomingtang had already made it's commitment to do this, and it was impossible for any one person to oppose and sabotage the peace negotiations. Being a high-level cadre of the Kuomingtang, I had all the more reason to obey. Otherwise, should not the leader of the party penalize me for violating party discipline?"

Marshall was surprised to hear this, but he did not seem to doubt my sincerity. I went on to tell him that before he came to China, I had indeed raised my objections to the Generalissimo about his mission. I then listed the three reasons I had given Chiang. I told Marshall that my main reason for thinking this way was that, in the past, I had frequent contacts with the Chinese Communists, especially Chou En-lai. I had come to the conclusion that the Communists were merely exploiting the Chinese people's mentality of being "tired of war after so many years of warfare" to instigate peace talks to gain time. They were not sincere and there would not be any good results.

I added: "Because I respect your position, I did not want you, a heroic figure in the world's eyes, to take on this mission that is bound to fail. At the very beginning, I had told the Generalissimo that anyone but Marshall could undertake this task. It is regrettable that those responsible for these diplomatic negotiations with our government have had hardly any contact with the Communists. They have no foresight, and yet they urge you to come and engage in this thankless task. What I worry about day in and day out is that, if the negotiations should fail, how can you step down with honor? for these reasons, when I met Mr.. Leighton Stuart in Shanghai I suggested to him that you must be prepared ahead of time. Today, I am delighted to be able to tell you in person what I have wanted to say. you should know that my objection to your assuming this mission was raised long before you came. In raising my objection I had only goodwill for you in mind. After you came I only hoped to be of help to you, but was given no opportunity. Now that I can see you in person, I cannot help but tell you all I know."

Marshall was very moved by what I told him. Realizing that he had been duped, he wanted me to go on talking. I repeated: "Chou En-lai's words were all fiction. The *New China Daily* has been stirring up trouble by planting rumors and hurling abuse at the government. The people are extremely disgusted with it. That day when the masses marched pass the *New China Daily*, someone upstairs threw down a teacup and hurt one of the marchers. The masses became so enraged they demolished the newspaper office. At that time I was chairing a meeting at the Ministry of Social Affairs. Who attended the meeting and when and where the meeting took place and all are on the record. How could I have the time to go to Chiao-ch'ang-kuo to direct the masses? If you do not believe me, you can ask those who attended the meeting and you find out that what I say is the truth."

Having heard all this, Marshall wanted to know the history of the breakups and make-up's between the Kuomingtang (KMT) and the Chinese Communist Party (CCP). I told him as much as I could remember. I also mentioned how I and Soviet Ambassador Bogomoloff deliberated over the Sino-Soviet Non-aggression Pact and how I, Chou En-lai, and Pan Han-nien discussed and decided on the statement of "Together We Confront the National Crisis" [*Kung-fu kuo-nan*] on September 22, 1937. Marshall showed great interest and was never bored with my narration. It was close to eight o'clock in the evening, time for his dinner engagement with Chiang. I wanted to stop, but Marshall urged me to go on, saying that it would be all right if he got to Chiang's residence a few minutes late.

Not wishing to disappoint him, I told him how, after the purge of 1927, I set up an investigation and statistical team modeled on the American FBI. high-level officials on the team had been in the United States studying engineering or science. Between 1927 and 1937, that activity was directly or indirectly under my supervision until I was appointed Minister of Education. That was the period when American technology defeated Soviet technology.

We uncovered more than a hundred communist underground units and about sixteen thousand Communists either defected to us or were captured, many of whom later were employed by the Kuomingtang at all levels and proved to be a good investment for us. (Chou En-lai himself told me that he was in Shanghai's International Concession then, and five minutes later he would have been captured by us.) Ku Shun-chang, head of the Communists' secret service, surrendered to us, which caused great fear among the Communists.

During the war, when I served as Minister of Education, all measures I adopted were designed to block the Communists from influencing our youth. Chou looked on me as his number one enemy. I was not surprised that he used all possible means to slander and smear me. I sincerely believed Communism was unsuitable for China as well as

America. And Chinese culture was much superior to that of the Soviet union. It is a culture that loves peace and it will make great contributions to the future world. I then quickly came to the conclusion: "Should you have any questions, please feel free to give me a ring." I said good-bye and left. This meeting lasted more than four hours, and I must have made an exceedingly deep impression on Marshall, as later events revealed.

I went to see Chiang and briefed him about my meting with Marshall. Chiang asked, "Has General Marshall ever invited you three to talk?" I said: "Never. This was the first time and I was the only one he invited." Only then did Chiang tell me that Marshall had misunderstood what I had told Stuart and that Chiang had suggested that Marshall should see me. Chiang thought that the reason Marshall had not interviewed the three of us on matters concerning the Kuomintang was that Marshall held preconceived ideas before he came to China. I recalled the first speech Marshall delivered in Chungking, and that fact was evident. The three of us were prevented from approaching Marshall. A distance had been created, which was a gross error. Furthermore, Communists were at Marshall's side, and their mission was to isolate Marshall from us. It was inevitable that Marshall's judgement was tainted, and he trusted the wrong side.

(I should record here that on August 15, 1964, at the request of the State Department, I met with U.S. officials at the Sheraton Hotel in New York City to discuss the question of "the loss of China." I stated that the failure of Marshall's mission weakened and isolated Chiang; at the same time the position of Mao Tse-tung in the Chinese Communist party was immensely strengthened.)

The San-min chui-i Youth Corps held its' Second National Congress in Lushan September 1-12, 1946. At the closing ceremony, Chiang gave a detailed speech analyzing the international situation to the entire membership. Afterward, he invited me to return with him to his official residence. He was visibly angry about Marshall's attitude. I took this opportunity to tell him that I had objected to Marshall's coming all along for precisely the same reason. Marshall wanted his mission to succeed and so had to accept the Communists' unreasonable demands and force us to accede to them. We had to endure and not quarrel with Marshall because the responsibility of any failed peace negotiations would fall on us. Should he leave empty-handed, Sino-American relations would be damaged, much to our disadvantage. Chiang listened to me in silence.

Not surprisingly, Marshall's mission did fail. The communist tactic of using the negotiations to gain time succeeded. In order to save Marshall's "face," President Truman had to think of some other reason for calling him back, so the White House announced he would be Secretary of State.

On January 8, 1947, when leaving China, Marshall issued a personal statement, the entire text of which was cabled from Washington, D.C., by the Central News Agency. It stated: "The greatest obstacle to peace in China has been the complete, almost overwhelming suspicion with which the Chinese Communist party and Kuomintang regard each other. On the one hand, the leaders of the government are strongly opposed to a communistic form of government. On the other, the Communists frankly stated that they are Marxists and intend to work toward establishing a communistic form of government in China, though first advancing through the medium of a democratic form of government of the American or British type. The government leaders are convinced in their minds that the communist-expressed desire to participate in a government of the type endorsed by the Political Consultative Conference last January had for its purpose only a destructive intention. The communists felt, I believe, that the government was insincere in its apparent acceptance of the Political Consultative Conference resolutions for the formation of the new government and intended to use coercion by military force and the action of secret police to obliterate the Communist party. Combined with this mutual deep mistrust was the conspicuous error by both parties of ignoring the effect of the fears and suspicious of the other party in estimating the reason for proposals of opposition regarding the settlement of various matters under negotiation."

Marshall had seen through the Communists; their insincerity as peace negotiators, their malice in creating difficulties, and their ultimate goal. Moreover, Marshall also stated that the "dominant group of reactionaries" in the Kuomintang had opposed every move he made to influence the formation of a coalition government.

Tillman Durdin, a newspaperman with the *New York Times* in China from 1930 to 1937, was closely in touch with Marshall, and for some time he assisted Marshall in an official capacity during Marshall's thirteen-month service as special envoy to China. Durdin came to see me and asked me what I thought of Marshall's statement. He believed that Marshall had me in mind when he made his statement. He also believed, and the *New York Times* reported, that I was regarded as "the civilian leader of the most uncompromising anticommunist wing of the Kuomintang." He asked for an interview. Informed about Durdin's intention, and wanting verbal precision, I asked my friend Li Wei-kuo to translate my comments on Marshall's statement of January 7, 1947, into English. The text was sent out by the Central News Agency in New York, and during the interview, I handed him a copy in person. The whole text appeared in the *New York Times*, January 14, 1947:

First of all, I wish to congratulate General Marshall for his achievements in fulfilling his mission since his arrival in China. He contributed much toward bringing together the various political parties, though it is regrettable that the Chinese Communist Party finally decided to abstain from participating in the National Assembly. He contributed toward expediting the successful convocation of the National Assembly, and above all, the adoption of what he described as a "democratic constitution which in all major respects is in accordance with the principles laid down by the all-party Political Consultative Conference of last January."

Secondly, I admire him for the insight he has shown in his study of the Chinese problem. I fully share his point of view on the Chinese Communist Party. If, however, he could have devoted a little more time in contacting members who take a leading part in the Kuomintang, his appraisal of the Chinese situation, in its proper breadth and depth, might have been more enlightening.

Thirdly, General Marshall is correct in pointing out that China's communist problem is different in character from that of the U.S. He is also right in warning the American public against the danger of evaluating the armed and powerful Chinese Communist Party by the standards used in evaluating small communist groups in America.

Fourthly, General Marshall shows remarkable knowledge in pointing out that the Chinese Communist Party is determined in conducting "a very harmful and immensely provocative" propaganda without regard for the facts, without any regard for the suffering of the people, and that they are equally determined in engineering the overthrow of the Government and the collapse of the national economy.

Fifthly, General Marshall is particularly sound in calling our attention to the fact that the Chinese communists are Marxists of the pure breed and "intend to work toward establishing a communistic form of government in China," and that in this sense they are a different species from agrarian reformers, as some Americans have unwittingly considered them to be.

Sixthly, I entirely agree with him on this thesis that China henceforth should bring about constitutional democracy by enforcing the new constitution and welcoming the minor political parties into the Government.

What is regrettable----and indeed a shame to us---is that General Marshall, a great friend from a great ally, in spite of his advanced age and in spite of hardships and pains, has labored and struggled in China's cause during the last 13 months and in the end has earned the distrust of a handful of the Chinese, that is the Chinese Communist Party. In the deliberate misrepresentation and abuse of the action, policies and purposes of the American Government the communist propaganda has been without regard for the truth, without any regard whatsoever for the facts, and has given plain evidence of a determined purpose of misleading the Chinese people and the world and to arouse a bitter hatred of Americans---it has been difficult to remain silent in the midst of such public abuse and wholesale disregard of facts, but a denial would merely lead to the necessity of daily denials, an intolerable course of action for an American official. When I read these sentences I could well imagine putting myself in his place, how painful and disillusioned at heart he must have been.

But to those who are familiar with communist tactics, it is not surprising at all. Is it not true that during the past 20 years the Chinese communists have every day been using the same method, and even more vehemently, against the Government of their own country and their own people? Have they not been purposely distorting the truth, misrepresenting the facts and indulging in vicious and abusive propaganda with the plain intention of misleading the Chinese people and the world and arousing a bitter hatred of the Chinese Government and Kuomintang? Take myself as an example. I was the first pioneer in blazing a trail for cooperation between the Kuomintang and the communists. In fact, I was the man who actually brought to consummation the plan of cooperation for the initial period. Yet today the one who has suffered most from their misrepresentation, insults and abusive tactics is none other than myself. In view of my own experience, anyone, accustomed to communist tactics, should not take their attacks on the U.S. as something unusual or surprising.

Most Kuomintang delegates in the National Assembly are persons who have either been schooled in Angle-American liberalism or influenced it. Unfortunately, they are the same persons who have been painted by communist propaganda as "reactionaries" or "die-hards." In point of fact, however, they are also the "liberals" who have adopted a democratic constitution which in all major respects "is in accordance with the principles laid down by the all-party Political Consultative Conference of last January." The communists are always masters in devising catchwords and slogans and in using them as deadly ideological weapons. They do so without the slightest moral scruples and with such persistence that people are unconsciously influenced and in the end take the thing at its face value. during the last 20 years, those who have uncovered or frustrated the communist plot of "establishing a communist form of government in China" have come under the label of "reactionaries and die-hards."

The study of political problems is the same as that of scientific problems. When a scientist approaches a problem of science, he must keep himself in close contact with the phenomena under study, and, by thoroughly investigating and analyzing all the relevant facts involved, discover the truth. The same method should be used in the study of the problems of politics. Staying [in] China for thirteen long months, possessed of immense wisdom and enthusiasm, and armed with a scientific method and mind, General Marshall, after careful study of the situation, has come to discover [that] "a very harmful and immensely provocative phase of the Chinese Communist Party procedure has been in the character of its propaganda" and that "the dyed-in-the-wool communists do not hesitate at the most drastic measures to gain their end."

Also it is no wonder that the General should have realized that the Chinese communists are Marxists of the pure breed and that their action and words are merely the means and policy with which to attain their ultimate aim of "establishing a communist form of government in China." So, while the democratic form of government of the American or British type" is the very ideal that the Kuomintang has been for years advocating and striving to achieve, this form of government, as General Marshall has rightly put it, is only a medium through which the Chinese Communist Party intends to ready its final goal.

I heard that the U.S. Embassy cabled the complete text of my afore-mentioned statement to Marshall. By then Marshall's understanding of me had become quite different from previous times. After he read my six-point reflections, he hopefully would no longer regard me as a "die-hard element" and a "reactionary."

In retrospect, the Communists' strategy was to divide the enemy. In Kwangtung they branded Hu Han-min as the rightist, Wang Ching-wei as the leftist; their tactic was to back the left and to condemn the right. After the Northern Expedition forces had taken control over the provinces south of the Yangtze River, they created terms like CC, Central Club, CC Clique, attacking my brother Kuo-fu and me in order to divide the Kuomintang's Central Executive Committee. Later they fabricated Chiang, Soong, Kung, and Ch'en as the Four Big Families [Ssu-ta chia-tsu] and made all kinds of false charges to malign those in the government. After the war of resistance against Japan broke out, they again tried to break up the Kuomintang by dividing it in "liberals" and "die-hard elements" and / or "reactionaries" because these people persisted in opposing communism and refused to be threatened or lured by the promise of gain. Those who were most virulently attacked by the Communists were actually the people whom the Communists feared the most. Since I had taken command of investigation and statistical work, I had been responsible for more than sixteen thousand Communists defecting. My policy during my tenure as Minister of Education had impeded communist expansion. Therefore, I naturally became the number one target of their attacks. But I had disciplined myself, and I was unassailable. All kinds of accusations only enhanced my reputation.

That reputation prompted Frederick Grain, China correspondent for the American magazine *Time*, to interview me in May 1947. I explained to him the main sources of Chinese culture were the I-Ching [Book of Changes] and Confucian philosophy, and I described in detain the history of nationalist-communist cooperation and split-ups. Little did I know that on the cover of *Time*, May 25, 1947, my portrait would appear, painted by Artzybasheff, a famous White Russian artist. The caption of the cover says "China's Ch'en Li-fu, the essence of life is the performance of benevolence." A three-and-a-half-page article described by thoughts, beliefs, personality, personal integrity, and achievements.

Grain reported that I "want the West to try to see China's problems through Chinese eyes." He continued that "when George Marshall, like many other Americans, last year suggested coalition with the communists, men like them were shocked (although Ch'en has been too correct to say so)." Grain suggested that "to Marshall and other Americans, communism still seems a distant threat. Ch'en and his friends have had the Reds breathing down their necks for 20 years. It has been war, bitter, open, accepted." I thought the tone was fair. Grain had not told me about the honor before the publication. Indeed, it was a surprise. As was customary, the original of the cover portrait was given to me as a gift. Such public display boosted my international reputation. The next year, [1948] when I visited the United States and Great Britain, those who received me often used my portrait on *Times* cover as a topic to begin a conversation. But within China, a number of people were quite unhappy and jealous of me.

++++++++

TWO OPPOSITES

MAO TSE-TUNG & CHIANG KAI-SHEK

by Bettis A. Garside, L.H.D.

Of six men who made the greatest impact on the history of the world during the middle half of the Twentieth Century - 1925 to 1975; each had an opportunity to make a dominant impression, not only on his own generation, but on future generations. In our judgement, three did leave the world a better place because of what they did, while three were "devils incarnate" whose paths were lined with suffering and slaughter.

Of the four men we have studied thus far, Churchill and Roosevelt will long be revered by a grateful world; while the names of Hitler and Stalin will be bitterly anathematized down the long corridors of the future.

Today we take a quick look as the last two of these historic six. For a short while they seemed to march along together, but they soon went in diametrically opposite directions....Mao Tse-tung and Chiang Kai-shek. They were born in neighboring provinces of mainland China; Chiang Kai-shek in Chekiang in 1886 and Mao Tse-tung in Hunan in 1893. As young men both men joined the revolutionary party of Sun Yat-sen, which in 1911 overthrew the harsh dynasty of the Manchus and founded the Republic of China. But there is no evidence that they were closely associated in their services to Dr. Sun.

Each, as a young man, came into touch with the Russian Communists, and had a good opportunity to observe Communism at first hand; but their reactions to their observations were diametrically opposite.

Chiang, the older of the two, was associated with the military from an early age. After youthful service as an enlisted man in the Chinese army, he attended Paoting, the "West Point of China." He then went to Japan and learned their military techniques at their Military College in Tokyo. Later, he went to Russia and observed Communism at first hand; and thereafter he was uncompromisingly opposed to Communism. Above all, in 1907 he became a disciple of Sun Yat-sen; and throughout his life he was a loyal follower of Dr. Sun's democratic philosophy.

On the other hand, while Mao Tse-tung also joined Sun Yat-sen's revolutionary party at an early age, he was always an enthusiastic supporter of Communism.

In the years immediately following Sun Yat-sen's overthrow of the Manchu Dynasty in 1911, the young Republic urgently needed guidance and assistance from other nations with well-established governments. Dr. Sun, who modeled his own political philosophy on our American government, turned to the United States for help and guidance. But we were too busy with own problems, especially our activities related to World War I, to give the struggling young Chinese republic anything more than our token sympathy. So Dr. Dun turned to the Russian communists, who eagerly embraced the opportunity to swing the new government of this vast nation into the communist orbit. In 1921, the Chinese Communist Party was founded, with Mao Tse-tung as its leader.

For the next six years Chiang and Mao cooperated as members of the Chinese Kuomintang Party, under the leadership of Sun Yat-sen. But after Dr. Sun's death in 1915, when the leadership of the Kuomintang fell on Chiang's shoulders, he soon discovered that the Communists were bent on seizing sole control of China. On March 14, 1927, a Communist faction led a bloody attack on Nanking, in which many lives were lost, including a number of Americans. Chiang's forces moved in, restored order in Nanking and drove out the Communists.

At that time Chiang could have completely obliterated the small Communist faction under Mao. But he allowed them to retreat into the northern mountains around Yenan. There, during the next decade, Mao built up the strength and influence of the Chinese Communist Party, largely through propaganda which pictured the Communists as an ultra-liberal and progressive party which would magically bring universal freedom, democracy and prosperity to all of China.

While Chiang was still a very young man, his family --- in accordance with Chinese custom---picked out a young Chinese woman as his wife. Absorbed as he was in his military duties and his close association with Sun Yat-sen, Chiang had little time for home life; but they had one son whom they named Ching-kuo. some years later they were divorced, though thereafter Chiang always provided for all her needs.

After Sun Yat-sen's death in 1925 Chiang succeeded to the leadership of the Kuomintang. He gathered around him a large group of patriotic and well-educated young Chinese leaders who were well versed in the democratic nations of the West. With their help, he instituted a broad and statesmanlike program of reform and modernization. He had fallen deeply in love with Meiling Soong, the youngest daughter of the remarkable Chinese tycoon Sam Jones Soong. But Meling's wise, strong-minded and staunchly Christian mother, Madame Soong, refused to let Meiling marry any man who was not a Christian. Chiang had come from a Buddhist and Confucian background, and while he had long had a respect for Christianity he had not formally professed that religion. He was too honest to profess anything unless he sincerely believed in it, even to win his Meiling. So he promised Madame Soong that he would made a careful study of Christianity to see whether he could profess his belief in it. After more than six months of earnest study, under the tutelage of a friendly American missionary, he did become a devoted and lifelong Christian. He and Meiling were married, and she remained a tower of strength and devotion to him as long as he lived.

Under President Chiang's leadership, between 1927 and 1937 the Chinese people enjoyed a decade of remarkable progress---politically---economically---socially and culturally. But on their eastern horizon there rose the darkening cloud of Japanese militarism, with its fantastic dream of bringing all of East Asia under its' domination.

While neither the peaceful nature of the Chinese people nor their limited economic resources permitted them to build up sufficient military strength to match Japan's overwhelming war machine, President Chiang put to good use his early military training, both in Japan and in Russia, to prepare China as fully as possible for the attack he knew was coming. When the Japanese, on July 7, 1937, attacked simultaneously both at the Marco Polo Bridge in Peking and by bombing Chinese vessels in Shanghai, Western military experts predicted that all of China would be conquered within a few months.

For eight long years the Chinese people suffered multi-millions of deaths and injuries at the hands of the Japanese invaders, and even more war-caused hunger and privation. As the war dragged on, American sympathy and admiration for the courageous Chinese people became more and more extensive; first through voluntary relief organizations such as United China Relief, then later through voluntary American forces such as Claire Chennault's Flying Tigers. And after the Japanese made their fatal mistake of a sneak attack on Pearl Harbor on December 7, 1941, Americans openly came to the military assistance of our Chinese allies.

Finally, eight years and a month after the Japanese militarists began their all-out attack on the Chinese people they realized they were hopelessly defeated, and America's atomic bombs brought the war to a shattering and humiliating end.

In Chiang Kai-shek's hour of victory, he would have been justified in demanding humiliating terms of surrender, and the imposition on the Japanese people of heavy burdens of post-war reparations. Yet at that point he did something unprecedented in history, and even now not full understood by the American people.

The sudden end of the war left large numbers of Japanese soldiers stranded in many parts of China---all of them dreading the wrath of the Chinese people whom they had been mercilessly slaughtering. But, to their amazement, President Chiang, instead of treating them harshly as prisoners of war, got this message to them:- "We are no longer enemies, but friends. You may keep all your personal belongings, and we will return you honorably to your homeland on Chinese vessels. Carry this message to your people:- "Now, let China and japan work together in friendship for the mutual welfare of our two countries, and for all of our neighboring countries in Asia." The Chinese sought no reparations from Japan.

By this unprecedented magnanimity Chiang Kai-shek captured the whole Japanese nation in peace as he could never have done in war. As long as he lived he was honored and beloved by the Japanese people, and when he died in 1975 Japanese tears were shed for him as freely as were those of his own countrymen.

Returning to developments in China, immediately after the end of the war there began a long chain of disastrous events which wiped out all of the postwar gains which the Chinese people had richly earned by eight ghastly years of warfare and suffering.

While the Communists under Mao Tse-tung had nominally been allies of the Nationalists during the war, and had demanded a generous share of all available war material and funds, they had actually done very little effective fighting against the Japanese and had hoarded much of their war material for use in the future. But throughout the war, and especially during its' closing years, they had carried on an extremely clever propaganda campaign, especially among the gullible Americans who were in China--- helpers in war relief organizations, missionaries, educators, business men---even the lower echelons in the American Embassy and Consulates. They mercilessly criticized the overburdened nationalists, both in civilian posts and in military service, for not doing more to meet all the needs of the Chinese people instead of concentrating on winning the war against japan. They promised that if <u>they,</u> the Communists, could get control, they would free the Chinese people from all restraints and would provide them with everything they could desire---without it costing anybody anything; and that they would bring "days of rejoicing" to the whole nation. So persuasive was this propaganda that it never occurred to anybody to ask <u>how</u> the Communists could do all these wonderful things for everybody, with no cost to anybody.

One can realize that many of the hungry, destitute and war-weary Chinese people might have grasped eagerly at this "pie in the sky." But it is hard to believe that intelligent and experienced Americans could have been so thoroughly brainwashed. But they set up a loud clamor that was echoed in all the communications we in New York were getting from our associates in China. Even more crucial, it was heard from the American Embassy in China to the State Department in Washington. Desperately needed funds which had been promised to the empty treasuries of the Nationalists were withheld; and war material urgently needed by the Nationalists to protect themselves from insurgent Communists were being held up in Washington for weeks and weeks on transparent excuses.

Finally, over the vehement protests of such responsible Americans as former American Ambassador Patrick Hurley, his successor Ambassador Leighton Stuart, and President Chiang's closest advisor, General Albert Wedemeyer, together with supporters of the Nationalists in both houses of Congress --- George Marshall was sent to China with an impossible ultimatum to President Chiang that he must either accept a subordinate position in a coalition with Mao Tse-tung or else he would lose all support from the American Government.

Faced by this intolerable situation, President Chiang once more succeeded in doing what everyone considered impossible. He gathered together all the remnants of his government and his military forces and withdrew to the war-devastated island of Taiwan. Once more, all the "excerpts" agreed he could neither establish a viable new government nor fend off the superior military strength which the Communists had built up --- with American encouragement and assistance. Instead, Chiang led both his own forces and the native Taiwanese in building up a peaceful, prosperous and power bastion of democracy on Taiwan.

When Chiang Kai-shek died at the age of 89 he was widely revered and sincerely mourned by all those who knew him in many nations around the world, He son, Chiang Ching-kuo was elected President of the Republic of China and today [1983] is worthily carrying on the leadership of Free China as his father's successor.

Meanwhile, on the mainland, Mao Tse-tung set up a harsh Communist government which at every point was the direct opposite of all the seductive propaganda he and his followers had been spreading immediately after the end of the war. Instead of the peace, democracy and prosperity they had promised, the entire mainland became --- and remained --- a vast poverty-stricken area. Instead of freedom for everybody, the populace was forced to live in communes where normal family life was impossible, children were alienated from their parents, and husbands were often separated from their wives.

All over mainland China, everyone who did not quickly submit to the Communists was subject to imprisonment, cruelty, even execution. The number of innocent victims slaughtered by the Chinese Communists under Mao Tse-tung are so staggering as to be incomprehensible. Just to quote a few authoritative estimates:- "The American Federation of Labor's Free Trade committee reported in December, 1952, of having received documented information showing more than 14,000,000 war prisoners and civilians massacred by the Chinese Communists." Another authentic source says:- "If the true figures were known from all areas of the country, the number of Chinese who perished at Red hands would be at least 30,000,000 (THIRTY MILLION) Whatever figure we accept, Communist sources along convict Red China of guilt for the greatest mass murder in history."

So, along with Adolph Hitler and Joseph V. Stalin, we must include Mao Tse-tung as a prime contender for the infamous title of "THE GREATEST MASS MURDERER IN HISTORY!"

+++++

Chapter II

PROSPECTS FOR CHINA

CHINESE PEOPLE SHOULD WALK TALL

IN THE 21st CENTURY

by Pei-Tsun Hau, LL.D. Former ROC Premier

China has a long history and a venerable culture. Throughout the world, the Chinese people are accorded respect. Our forefathers had three great inventions: the compass, gunpowder and printing. The compass, however, did not lead China to gain sovereignty over the seas. Gunpowder did not transform China into a superpower. And, printing did not reduce the number of illiterate people in China.

A Century and a Half of Misfortune

A series of unequal treaties, starting with the 1842 Treaty of Nanking and ending with the 1900 Treaty of Peking, humiliated the Chinese by forcing them to surrender many of their sovereign rights, to cede much of their territory, and to pay massive indemnities. Yet, if the 19th century marked the beginning of the Chinese people's nightmare, then the first half of the 20th century made it even more terrifying. domestic distress and repeated foreign aggression led to the impoverishment of the farmers, the universality of illiteracy, the complete lack of modern knowledge, and the backwardness of technology.

Chinese people reacted in one of two extreme ways: one segment of the society worshipped all things foreign and fawned on foreigners, while another segment looked down on and opposed all foreign influence. Somewhere between these two extremes, the Chinese people lost their self-confidence.

Throughout China, men of learning sought solutions to this sad state of affairs. Examples include the Ching Dynasty's Westernization movement and Dr. Sun Yat-sen's national revolution. from their failures in that painful age, our intellectuals gradually learned that China needed democracy and science. Later on, they also realized that China needed ethics and a strong economy as well. The reasoning was that science could be used to save the nation, democracy could be used to govern the nation, ethics could be used to stabilize the nation, and a strong economy could make the nation prosper.

The main activity in China during the first half of the 20th century (from 1900 to 1949), however, was not the implementation of democracy, the advancement of technology, or the promotion of national development. The most important activity was the waging of war. This experience taught us an invaluable lesson, namely that frequent uprisings and wars destabilized China and prevented national development. For China, all that war would lead to was fruitless struggles in the shadow of poverty and backwardness.

So then, just what kind of century for mankind has the 20th century been? The famed American scholar Arthur Schlesinger Jr., one-time advisor to President John F. Kennedy, described the 20th century as an age of victory and of tragedy. There has been glory, and there has been suffering. There have been expectations, and there have been disasters. There have been anger, blood, and cruelty, and there have been great heroism, hopes, and dreams. In short, the 20th century has been a century of war, and China, of all nations, has suffered the most and the longest from war's calamitous effects.

Taiwan and the Chinese Mainland

In the second half of the 20th century, the people in Taiwan and the people in the Chinese mainland have lived under completely different systems, and thus they have met with two entirely different fates. The Chinese mainland has been ruled by communism, while Taiwan has been prospering under Dr. Sun Yat-sen's Three Principles of the People.

Many friends of mine who have visited the Chinese mainland tell me that they have very strong and contradictory feelings about it. They love its rivers and hills, but cannot stand its' political institutions; they love the great expanse of land, but find it difficult to put up with its backwardness.

My friends tell me that, when visiting the mainland, one can see geographical China with its' Yangtze and the Yellow Rivers. They say one can glimpse historical China with its' Great Wall and the city of Xian. And, they say one can find cultural China in the displays of the Palace Museum and in the Dunhuang Caves. But, my friends also say that over there one cannot find a democratic and free China with an equitable distribution of wealth. The Republic of China in the Taiwan Area, after forty some years of hard work, provides a sharp contrast to the Chinese mainland.

How did the ROC on Taiwan raise its' per capita GNP from below US $200 to over US$10,000? On the whole, this growth may be attributed primarily to government policies that guaranteed political and social stability and provided conditions favorable to development. Of course, many a economic factor was also involved. first was the government's basic pursuit for a very pragmatic market-oriented economic policy. Second, the people of Taiwan, and especially small and medium-size enterprises, made the most of their energy and potential. Third, most Taiwan laborers are well-educated, industrious and, since they are motivated by profit, very efficient.

The year 1988 was a very meaningful for Taiwan, and we should all look back on that year with pride. In 1988, the per capita income of Taiwan exceeded US $6,000. At that time, any area or country with a per capita income of more than US $6,000 was considered a "high-income area." In Asia, only Japan, Hong Kong, Singapore, and the Republic of China on Taiwan were ranked within the world's top twenty-six high-income nations or economies.

In those days, the ROC on Taiwan was constrained diplomatically, saddled with high military expenditures, pinched by shortage of natural resources, and challenged by global competitors, and yet, we were able to overcome each of these problems in the end.

Apart from the government policies, the efforts of small and medium-sized businesses, and the top-notch labor force noted above, another factor that has contributed to Taiwan's economic success has been our economic system. It has made investors happy to invest, savers happy to save, workers happy to work, and talented persons happy to put their talents to good use. The "great rice bowl" of communism in the Chinese mainland had the opposite effect. There everybody was paid the same whatever their contribution, and intellectuals were looked down upon. There were such slogans as "raising pigs is better than teaching school" and "better a barber than a surgeon." It is hard to imagine any country or any society becoming a modern nation without respecting its intellectuals. Professor Fang Lizhi once said in all seriousness, "The Chinese communist authorities like science, but not scientists."

The Pride and Apprehensions of Taiwan

After forty odd years of hard work, we on Taiwan have earned a measure of respect worldwide for our success. We have achieved universal education, stable prices, and relatively high economic growth, large amounts of foreign reserves, and a high rate of private savings. stated another way, Taiwan's "Economic Miracle," which was forged over four decades, has been the product of political and social stability in times of crisis and the coordinated effort of the public and private sectors.

It was thus with great pride that we passed through three important economic thresholds in 1992. The ROC's GNP exceeded US $200 billion that year, ranking twentieth largest worldwide. The ROC's per capita GNP exceeded US $10,000 in 1992, ranking twenty-fifth worldwide. And, the ROC's trade exceeded US $150 billion in 1992, ranking fourteenth worldwide. Moreover, the ROC's foreign exchange reserves have hovered around US $85 billion in recent years, first or second highest in the world.

I must, however, point out that behind these indices lurk many phenomena that require immediate remedies. For example, private investment is insufficient. Industrial upgrading is lagging behind real needs. Public debt is expanding. The influence of special interest groups is spreading. Real estate prices are high, and there is a widening gap between the rich and the poor.

If we widen our vision, we find that we need to improve our living environment, cultural activities, and social peace. This is why the administration should focus on long-term and integrated planning and development, and should emphasize social justice and stability.

At this grand gathering, let me frankly list some of the psychological obstacles and other bottlenecks that we must break through in promoting Taiwan's development; (1) short-sightedness, (2) over emphasis on individual and particular interests, (3) deep-rooted regionalism, (4) a high regard for special privilege, (5) no understanding of the rule of law, and (6) insufficient consensus and solidarity.

Thoughts on the Overall Situation

How will Chinese people handle things in the quickly approaching 21st century? To answer this question, let me first outline five major trends in the next century.

First, the threat of a full-scale nuclear war will gradually disappear. Basically, the 21st century will be a time of peace, but small-scale military conflicts will still be unavoidable. **Second**, communism everywhere is on the decline. Democracy and market economics are being embraced around the world. Basically, the 21st century will be a time of democracy. **Third,** regional economic cooperation will gradually increase. While the economic gap between East and West Hemispheres will shrink, the economic differences between North and South will increase. **Fourth**, advanced technology and information will play a leading role in the world. **Fifth,** environmental consciousness will spread round the globe.

Chinese people everywhere should reflect on the overall situation in light of the long-term interests and the continued development of the Chinese people. They should spare no effort to enhance the quality of democracy and maintain the competitiveness of the national economy.

I am confident that success or failure depends on the scope of one's vision. Let us not tarnish our glorious future with narrow-minded and impractical ideas today.

The government is responsible for developing the Republic of China into a more open, democratic, and progressive nation, and thereby establishing a good model for China's future development. This coincides with the five major administrative goals that I promoted during my term as Premier---stability, democracy, rule of law, development and unification.

We realize that only through stability can we survive. Only through democracy can we develop. Only through the rule of law can we be fair. Only through development can we move ahead. Only through national unification can we have a future.

Having devoted a lifetime to military service, I changed to civil service just three years ago. My experiences in office taught me that accelerating democratization is easy, but improving the quality of democracy is not.

When I was serving in the army, some people described me as a "strong man." In fact, all I ever did was do my duty with a strong will. Under the ROC system, it is impossible for a soldier to seize political power. While, political elites and opinion leaders in the West often worry about coup d'etats in developing countries, such an unacceptable way of attaining ruling power could never happen in our society.

Nevertheless, I would like to remind my friends around the world that we should worry about "money politics," which degrades democracy as much as a military coup does. What I am referring to is wealthy people trying to win the elections by illegal means, taking advantage of legal loopholes, or even bribing voters with the behind-the-scenes assistance of interest groups. Owing to the large financial gap between some candidates, it has been very difficult for capable, moral, experienced, but penny-pinched candidates to win elections. Under such circumstances, democracy has become an activity for big business and professional bureaucrats. This is worrisome.

If seizing political power with bullets is to be condemned, then using silver bullets to win an election is equally unforgivable. We find that to fend off real bullets is easy, but to guard against silver bullets is difficult.

Personally I believe that the quality of democracy in Taiwan can be brought close to the standard of modern Western countries only through the checks and balances party politics, persistent demands for clean elections by the whole people, and strict supervision by public opinion.

I often compare economic development to a train running on a two-way track. The train can speed up, slow down, or even go in reverse. Democracy, howe4ver, is like a train on a one-way track. It must move only forward, never backward. "Moving forward" refers both to the speed of democratization and to the quality of the democracy achieved.

China will have no right to speak in the International arena if it does not have any economic strength. In recent years, some scholars have come up with the concept of "economic China" to combine the economic advantages of mainland China, Taiwan, Hong Kong, and Macau. We should give deep thought to this idea.

Personally I believe that China will have no hope if the mainland does not reform, and Taiwan will have no future if the two sides of the Taiwan Straits do not have any exchanges. From Taiwan's point of view, "economic China" is very attractive in many respects. It would enhance investment opportunities, relieve tensions resulting from economic and industrial upgrading, regulate production activities in different areas, demonstrate examples of reforms, and benefit each of the major regions in China. These factors can sharpen China's competitive edge as it develops economically in the 21st century.

In a market economy, maintaining a favorable competitive edge is crucial to the development of a country. Low prices, high quality products, and after-sale service are the three features that provide competitive edge. Quality is the result of science, ethics, law, and discipline. Only a high quality humane society (**one that adheres to ethics and the rule of law**) can produce high quality economic goods.

Conclusion

Taiwan and the Chinese mainland will need each other in the coming century. Chinese people around the world are responsible for each other. To improve democracy in Taiwan and to democratize mainland China in appropriate ways as it reforms economically requires the wisdom of leaders on both sides of the Taiwan Straits.

The 20 million people in Taiwan today should have a deep affinity for Taiwan but should not distinguish between *pen-ti-jen* and *wai-shen-jen*. We live together and share a common destiny, and we should cherish a deep affection for each other as we jointly develop Taiwan into a highly democratic, healthy, and prosperous society. Chinese people around the world should keep their "Chinese" minds open. With the Chinese mainland ever in our hearts, we should cooperate with the mainland and seek to transform it. At this historic moment, outstanding overseas Chinese who serve in U.S. enterprises should participate in the great project of modernizing and democratizing China.

I am confident that, by combining our deep affinity for Taiwan with the broad-mindedness of all Chinese, the reforms in the Chinese mainland, and the examples of other regions will eventually allow all 1.2 billion Chinese people to **walk tall in the 21st century.**

A PREVIEW OF CHINA'S POLITICAL, MILITARY AND ECONOMIC DEVELOPMENTS IN THE POST - DENG XIAOPING ERA

by Jacob K. J. Ma

Although DENG XIAOPING hasn't breathed his last yet, his health remains so frail and vulnerable that he can no longer have much impact on the Chinese Communist regime. It's conceivable that the post-Deng era has already begun.

The logical question now is: will there be changes in the post-Deng China? Will there be chaos? This question, it'd seem, ccan be answered thusly: That there's be changes...changes in all spectrums of life and society. After more than four decades of communist rule in China, it has come to a stage that there is universal demand for change. None-the-less, from the standpoint of imminent developments in the situation, the changes will be gradual, piecemeal, and evolutionary, rather than drastic and all-out. This, it can be said that within this short period of time, any turmoil will be small ones, and there won't be overwhelming upheavals in mainland China.

In the post-Deng Chinese communist regime, there is bound to be a transitional period dominated by the so-called "Jiang (Zemin) leadership," and that stage may run into 1997 when the sovereignty of Hong Kong is scheduled to be transferred to China, an event that could have great consequences to the mainland. In that same year, the 15th National Congress of the Chinese Communist Party will be held, providing a crucial opportunity for the adjustment of political power. It'll be seen that in the past, all important personnel changes have been effected by the party's congress, as a result of struggles for power.

Now, it may be asked why would there be a transitional period in the Chinese communist regime after Deng? The reason is that following the departures of two generations of strongmen: Mao Zedong and Deng Xiaoping from China's political stage, there hasn't been any leadership person of the third generation who possessed the experience and prestige in the party and the military to qualify for the "strongman" of the new generation. This included Jiang Zemin who still lacks the prestige and authority and who time has not ripened yet. the second reason is that ;amongst the chieftains of the various factions in the communist hierarchy, they realize that in the absence of the qualifications and prestige for themselves to reach the top summit it'd be best, with a view to protecting the regime and solidifying the dictatorship, to maintain some sort of collective leadership under "Jiang as the nucleus."

However, it will be seen that a period of transformation is a period of transition, and so it can't but be temporary in its' character. In this context, power struggles would be inevitable, under the disguise of superficial solidarity. This is especially true in Jiang's position. In order to build up his core leadership, he must tackle with the challenges of his rivals and dissidents, and resort to diverse tactics to beat and eliminate them, so that after the period of transition is over, he'd emerge as the nation's strongman and supreme leader.

Let's analyze briefly some of the political, military and economic changes that could take place in the post-Deng era in China:

Politically, the highest leadership wielding real power is comprised of the seven standing members of the Central Political Bureau; namely: Jiang Zemin, Li Peng, Giao Shir, Li Ruihuan, Hu Qintao, Zhu Ronqi, and Liu Hwaqing. Among these seven, Qiao Shi enjoys the highest seniority in the party. He has headed the party's political intelligence system, and a person known for his enlightened style, he is currently the chairman of the National People's Congress, and enjoys the support of the elder statesmen. Long before Zhao Ziyang's ouster, it was reported that he might be Zhao's successor, being the only person that could challenge Jiang Zemin. It has been whispered in Beijing recently to the effect that **"with the ebb of river [meaning Jiang], so will the rock [meaning Qiao Shi) surface."** This testifies to his popularity in the minds of the public. however, in as much as Qiao's more inclination towards prudence and introversion, he won't be easily tempted to adventure until the circumstances become completely favorable. Under the pretext of "anti-corruption" campaign, Jiang has recently taken action to liquidate Zhen Xidong of the so-called "Beijing Gang." Succeeding Zhen as the party secretary of the municipality of Beijing is Wei Qianxin who, together with Qiao Shi, used to belong to Hu Yaopang's faction. Wei's appointment to the Beijing portfolio came through Qiao's recommendation. That Jiang has taken Qiao's suggestion seems to confirm the belief that collaboration between these two powerful personages in the post-Deng era has laid the foundation for political stability during the period of transition.

Even before the event cited above, Jiang Zemin had begun his efforts to win over the associates of the late Hu Yaopang. In last March, he took advantage of his visit to Jiangsi Province to pay respects to Hu Yaopang's grave, and upon the request of Hu's widow, he agreed to set up a stone tablet inscribed with these laudatory words: *"Brilliant and Frank, Unselfish and Altruistic."* It transpired that the widow, nee Ms. Li Zhao, had requested this posthumous honor six years ago after her husband's passing, but no action was taken. Hu was widely respected by the young intellectuals, but the conservative diehards stigmatized him for his "capitalistic liberalism." He was dismissed eventually, and the "1989 Democracy Movement" by Beijing students was unleashed to commemorate him. In aligning himself with Hu's followers, it's Jiang Zemin's purpose: first, to hit back against the pressures of the elder conservative leaders; second, to checkmate the resurgence of Zhao Ziyang's influences; and third, to win over the goodwill of the intellectuals, thereby ameliorating the assaults of the democracy movement.

In the realm of military affairs, it will be recalled that since the first plenary meeting of the 14th Congress of the Chinese Communist party held in October 1992 and the 8th National People's Congress held in March 1993, Jiang Zemin has, under the auspices of Deng Xioping, taken over military power from the "Yang family's generals. "Yang Shangqun, an elder statesman reputed as the "Dragon Head" of the Yang hierarchy of family generals had, over the years, successively relinquished his eminent offices which included: standing member of the Central Political Bureau (politburo), and President of the People's republic of China (PRC). His younger sibling whose name is Yang Baipin, was also relieved of his post as director of the General Political Department. With Deng's patronage, Jiang Zemin garnered the coveted appointment as chairman of the Central Military Committee, thereby enabling him to make important appointments, to decided on promotions of military ranks, and to step up political training in the military system.

Taking advantage of his new powers, he has since issued the "decision to strengthen party development in the army," and enjoined that at all times, the military should obey the party and take orders from the Central Military Committee recently, it was decided to place all armed police units in China under the dual leadership of the Central Military Committee and the State Council (Cabinet). In this way, Jiang has garnered additional authority in selecting and appointing police cadres. Moreover, thanks to Deng's assistance, Jiang has won over the collaboration of Liu Hwaqing, a standing member of the Politburo, and of Zhang Zhen, another deputy chairman of the Central Military committee. As a result of these maneuvers, it has helped Jiang Zemin tremendously in the military arena. He has had no military experience or credentials to speak of, but as most of the senior military leaders had passed away, there are no strong rivals to challenge Jiang. It is conceivable that for a short period in the post-Deng transition, there won't be any serious problems in the military sphere.

On the economic side, the problems for Jiang Zemin appear to be even more troublesome, and they pose greater tests and challenges to him than what he has encountered in the political and military situation. In the last several years, under the open economic policies advocated by Deng Xieoping, salient achievements have been made, such as in the field of attracting foreign, overseas Chinese, and Taiwanese investments, and bringing about a high and phenomenal rate of economic growth. On the other hand, however, problems have arisen in mainland China's industry and agriculture.

Concerning the problem of agriculture, it may be pertinent to refer to the speech by Dien Qiyun at the national People's Congress in March. He pointed out, in his capacity as deputy chairman of that congress, that among the 10 articles announced by Premier Li Peng on agricultural reform, "the most important, fundamental, and crucial one is to apply the rules of market economy to guide agricultural production.... Instead of sacrificing agriculture to develop industry, which has resulted in exploiting the peasants, and rendering it impossible for China's agriculture to catch up with industry over the past decades."

He said further that China's agricultural policy has consistently run counter to the laws of value. He warned that unless this problem is resolved, we won't be able to rule the country much longer. What Dien Qiyun said about the agricultural problem is really most insightful and pertinent. In consequence of the shortfall of farm production, "food certificates" have been revived in 29 of the 35 mammoth and medium-size metropolises in China since last winter. Also, the agricultural downturn has caused China's rural population to flock to urban areas, spawning what is branded as a "blind flow." Incidentally, this desperate need for peasants to struggle for subsistence constitutes a serious social problem.

One grave problem in the industrial area is that most of the state (government) operated industries have failed in recent years. As the backbone of industrial production, state enterprises are the products of the communist regime's monopolistic and planned economy. Since the regime is now committed to developing industries in keeping with the principles of market economy, enterprises with foreign, overseas Chinese and Taiwanese investments, as well as joint ventures, have steadily flourished.

On the contrary, state enterprises, as a rule, have fallen into the abyss of deterioration, incurring huge losses. Under these circumstances, it's now imperative for China's state enterprises to change their patterns of operation by instituting some reform or overhaul, or even by closing down. But how to proceed and what to do?

Anent this paradoxical issue, it appears that among the authorities in mainland China, there is still wishful thinking that planned economy and free market economy could coexist, by embellishing the former as "socialist market economy."

In light of the anomalous situation, and if the Chinese communist regime really intend to resolve, fundamentally, the industrial and agricultural problem now confronting it, the only viable policy will be to restore private ownership of land to the peasants and to admit the production and marketing of farm products in the orbit of market economy. It will also be necessary to privatize state enterprises in order to establish a comprehensive system of market economy. But can this be practical under communist rule? Would Jiang Zemin have the stamina and resolve to get involved in such basic issues? This is why economic problems will pose the greatest challenges to the "Jiang leadership" during the transition in the post-Deng era.

Now, during the period of transition, all kinds of changes might occur, and a series of power struggles are bound to be waged, openly or sub rosa, until the transition comes to its' end. By then, two kinds of antipodal scenarios would ensue: one being that a new strongman emerges who will keep communist dictatorship; the other being that mainland China will progress towards democracy and constitutional government...to the greatest happiness of the Chinese nation, and to usher in the prospects of national unification.

It may be mentioned here that in February this year [1996], the U.S. department of Defense published a report on the possible developments in post-Deng China, representing the researches conducted by scholars and specialists. Almost at the same time, a research group in Japan, under the name of "International Forum," presented a report to Premier Murayama on the same subject matter. In both documents, they expressed the view that the Chinese regime may continue to practice dictatorship or may incline gradually towards democracy and opening. They also envisage a **third** alternative, in that there will be internal disruption, as the central governments loses its control and "local barons" spring up, thereby creating tremendous turmoil's and disorder.

It's the view of this writer that the chances for the last mentioned situation appear to be, judging by what has been said above, very slight and minimal.

++++++

PERCEPTIONS OF THE REPUBLIC OF CHINA'S EDUCATION TOWARDS THE 21st CENTURY

A Preface

by Wei-fan Kuo, Ph.D.
ROC Minister of Education

In less than five years, we are going to step into the Twenty-First century. Times change and what is normal today may be radically changed tomorrow. We must be prepared to live in a different world, the roots of which we experience today. When we look forward to the future, we need to envision ourselves as being on a speeding train where the scenes flick by at amazing speed. Gradually we develop a feeling that an embryonic, future society is forming.

In the Twenty-First century, advanced technology will bind countries and people closer together. Even though countries vary in their national consciousness and traditional philosophies regarding their sovereign rights, internationalization cannot be stopped. We people in Taiwan will travel abroad more frequently in the future. Mass media informs us of news, sports and entertainment programs just the same as they are experienced by other countries. High-tech communications thus squeeze the world into a globalized neighborhood. The links between Taiwan, (R.O.C.) and mainland China, conceivably, will be expanded and upgraded. When the Republic of China has fulfilled its long-range plans to establish an Asia-Pacific Regional Operations Center and National Information Infrastructure---when they are a reality---then the R.O.C. will be truly entwined with the international network. Our educational system has to change to meet the needs of the Twenty-First century. The learning environment in the Twenty-First century is not illusory or imaginary but it poses a clear picture of what the new century will encompass. We need to adjust our developmental strategies for educational planning in order to be prepared for the coming challenges.

Japan has formed a committee for educational reforms for the Twenty-First century. The United States has issued plans and strategies to examine and review plans for educational projections aimed toward the Twenty-First century. Likewise, Korea has established an Educational Reform Committee to survey the needs of educational reform for the future. These movements indicate that the new age requires new education and this will be followed by a new society. However, history leads us to know that educational development has advanced in a steadily-continuing progression. Educational reforms can't be instigated momentarily; it requires a developing, evolutionary process. Plans for educational reform need to be applied continuously and sequentially in order to avoid complete chaos in the approaching millennium.

During the long rule of the Chou Dynasty, government officials foresaw the need for change and, there, instituted and revised their own existing programs and government schemes to meet the challenge of the New Age.

This report is the first volume of our perception of the educational needs of the Twenty-First century. Its purpose is to provide information about how education departments consider educational reforms for those people who care about educational development. It also replies to the public query as to where our educational system will be pointed in the near future. However, this document cannot be considered as official policy because it has not be accepted formally or proclaimed procedurally by the authorities. It is merely a public report, the outcome of discussion and committee conferences. It is used to expose a multitude of knowledgeable concepts and ideas. This treatise is designed with the intention of eliciting tactics and schemes concerned with the needs of tomorrow from those people concerned and involved with education in our Republic. This may also be thought of as a point of reference for educational policy-making and policy implementation. The Ministry of Education, in publishing this report, looks forward to a greater degree of consensus between government and the public on the main direction of educational reform.

We look forward to opinions not only from professional educators, but also from the committees of the Council for Educational Reform. When the second volume of this report---perhaps two years in the future---is published, more schemes may be developed and inaugurated.

The original ideas for this book were the major conclusions made by the Seventh National Educational Conference in June 1994. It is the product of those conferees; thinking, debating and discussing in groups and committees. Based on the results of their recommendations, the Ministry of Education established nine special teams to examine certain key subjects in an in-depth, intensive way. Later on, the Educational Research Committee and the National Institute of Resources and Researches invited experts and scholars to discuss the conclusions arrived at by the special teams. Those conclusions as well as the drafts from the different departments and related educational groups were essential components of the report. The composition and structure of the report were reviewed and polished into presentable form. The report is composed of twelve chapters. The first chapter is the 'Proceedings' of the whole report. It discusses and reviews present conditions---the status quo. The other eleven chapters are devoted to educational tactics and potential solutions in various fields. The main thrust of this report is concerned with alleviating student examination pressure and encouraging educational liberalization. The last part of the book is a view of the future in education along with a chapter summary to bring a cohesiveness to the total theses. Since this is the first such report by the Minister of Education, it is requested that readers be tolerant of possible errors of omission or conception. Any criticisms of this work will be incorporated in the course of preparing future reports.

+++++

THOUGHTS on ROC SOVEREIGNTY

by Bernard T.K. Joei, Ph.D.

Recently, the question of the international-law status of the islands of Taiwan and the Pescadores, and consequently that of the Republic of China, has been raised by some separatist movement members, as it was during and since World War II by world powers. Different theories about the concept of sovereignty over these islands were held by scholars during that time, each arguing the case from different angles. Several of the pertinent ones are worth reviewing briefly.

It is true that, in the 1950's, the governments of the United Kingdom, Canada and even the United States, because of international politics, all expressed an ambiguous attitude concerning the ROC's sovereignty over Taiwan and its islands.

Nevertheless, the sovereignty of the Republic of China over Taiwan and the Pescadores does not depend on recognition by other nations. Such sovereignty is supported, among other things, by the principle of *uti possidetis* of international law. The esential element of (A) the intention and will to act as sovereign, and (B) an actual exercise or display of such authority. These factors were both manifestly present in the ROC's occupation of the islands, especially after the government moved to Taipei from the Chinese mainland in 1949.

What makes the sovereignty issue complex is that Taiwan has been under the governance of three different sovereign governments over the past 200 years or so, mostly serving as hinterland for the last Imperial Chinese dynasty, the Ch'ing, until the island was declared the 22nd Province of China in 1885. Only ten years later, Taiwan and the adjacent Pescadores were ceded to Japan by the Ch'ing government with the signing of Treaty of Shimonoseki. Thus, Taiwan was not legally Chinese territory for 50 years until the defeat of japan in 1945. As one of the allied powers fighting Japan throughout the Pacific War, the ROC, then the sovereign successor to the Imperial Ching Dynasty of China, regained possession of Taiwan and the Pescadores from Japan in 1945, along with other territory on the Chinese mainland illegally occupied by Japan between 1931 and 1945.

When the Chinese communists occupied the Chinese mainland in 1949 and declared the People's Republic of China, the ROC government relocated to Taiwan while continuing its "effective occupation" begun in 1945.

This "effective occupation" can also be legally described in terms of the principle of acquisitive prescription or usucapion. This principle, according to French international lawyer Nguyen Quoc Dinh, **"allows the acquisition foreign territory** (as Taiwan was technically to the ROC in 1945, despite originally being Chinese territory) **by a State** (in this case, the ROC) **exercising its authority over that territory in unbroken and pacific manner throughout a long period of time. Through usucapion, the ownership acquired in good faith is transformed into the right of sovereignty."**

By 1952, an additional legal principle affirming ROC sovereignty over Taiwan and the adjacent Pescadores came into effect when the Japanese Peace Treaty was signed, on April 28, 1952, Japan thereby relinquished sovereignty over Taiwan and other lands mentioned in the treaty. This dereliction, as it is called in international law, rendered the area concerned *terrae nullius*, subject to acquisition by another power---in this case, the Republic of China.

The separate Treaty of Peace between the republic of China and Japan, likewise dated April 28, 1952, recognizes that Japan has renounced all rights, title, and claim to Taiwan and other adjacent islands. Hence there is no question of the ROC having sovereignty over Taiwan by this date.

The above theory is supported by many other international lawyers, such as Hubert Thierry, Charles Rousseau, to mention only a few. In view of the above and taking the fact into account that there is "peaceful and continuous display of State authority" by the central government of the Republic of China on Taiwan since 1949, the sovereignty of the Republic of China is affirmed once and for all beyond any shadow of a doubt.

Now that the issue of the ROC's sovereignty over Taiwan is settled, the ROC's statehood can not be questioned either, according to international law. The Republic of China definitely satisfies the four characteristics of a State set out by the Montevideo Convention of 1933 on the Rights and Duties of States in its' Article 1 as follows:

The state as a person on international law should possess the following qualifications: **(A) a permanent population; (B) a defined territory' (C) a government, and (D) a capacity to enter into relations with other States.**

Even though the "permanent population" and "defined territory" of the ROC underwent profound changes between 1945 and 1949, Taiwan became a part of the ROC in 1945 and remained so in 1949, despite the loss of the remaining territory and population. Thus, the Republic of China on Taiwan, established in 1912, has continuously existed as a State since then and has possessed the four characteristics above, so it is indeed a state in the full sense of the term according to international law.

The fact that the ROC is not recognized diplomatically by all states internationally, does not affect its being a state or political entity enjoying a status of international person in terms of international law.

As a "political entity" is something of factual existence, it requires no further recognition; whether or not it is recognized does not affect the *de facto* existence of this very "political entity." Therefore, even if Beijing does not recognize the Republic of China as a "political entity," this is surely insufficient to obscure the fact that this political entity does indeed exist.

This political entity called Republic of China is part of China which has been divided since 1949. The fact is that China has been divided since 1949 into two political entities; The PRC on Chinese mainland and the ROC on Taiwan. Neither Beijing nor Taipei can be entitled to represent alone the whole of China.

This is immediately clear when we apply the same sovereignty test to Beijing's PRC. The PRC did not exist in 1931-1945, so it was not of the allied powers to whom Japan surrendered in 1945. The PRC did not exist in 1945, so it could not "effectively occupy" Taiwan then, nor claim acquisitive prescription over Taiwan because it did not exist itself then. In 1949, when the PRC was proclaimed, it never exerted any authority over Taiwan, nor did it occupy Taiwan in any way. Finally, the PRC was not in possession of Taiwan in 1951 when Japan signed the main Peace Treaty on September 8 that year in San Francisco, nor did it conclude a separate Treaty of Peace in 1952. Thus, the PRC can hardly claim to represent people and territory of Taiwan to which it has never had any sovereign claim at any time.

The legal implications of this are profound, indeed. Specious claims by the PRC of sovereignty over Taiwan have led some to mistakenly conclude that should the Chinese communists invade Taiwan or intervene in Taiwan affairs, such a situation would be construed as an "internal PRC problem about which the international community [including the United States] could do little." In truth, according to international law, military intervention or action against Taiwan by the PRC would be action against a "foreign" territory, and subject to all the international implications thereof.

While the complex history of the past century can not be undone, the ROC believes that "Humpty-Dumpty can be put back together again," and China can be reunited. Both Beijing and Taipei have the same "one China" goal. Therefore the two sides of the Taiwan Strait must identify with the other. The two political entities of different sizes but equal status must co-exist within the framework of the Chinese ethnic, historical and cultural nation.

Consequently, mutual sincerity and mutual trust must be built up gradually between the two parties through peaceful means, so that a thoroughly democratic re-unified China can be eventually achieved in a harmonious atmosphere.

"ONE CHINA"
or
"ONE TAIWAN, ONE CHINA"?

Question of Re-admitting the Republic of China to

the United Nations

by Charles C. M. Chung

Last December [1995], the Foreign Affairs Committee of the Legislative Yuan in Taiwan adopted a resolution submitted by Mr. C.Y. Lee (organizer of the Alliance for the realization of one Taiwan and one China) for presentation to the Plenary Session of the Legislative Yuan for consideration. According to Mr. Lee, it is the belief of the Alliance that, in order to regain a seat in the United Nations, the government of Taiwan should relinquish a "One China" policy and adopt a "One Taiwan, One China" position. He appealed to the National government to discard the idea of "One nation with two UN seats" and apply for admission to the United Nations as a new member. He further indicated that it would be absolutely impossible to be re-admitted under the name "Republic of China" or "Republic of China on Taiwan." On the other hand, it might be more feasible to be admitted as a new member under the name Taiwan.

Veto Power Under UN Charter Precludes This Route

Not so. contrary to Mr. Lee's proposal, Taiwan's application as a new member is absolutely impossible under the provisions of the UN Charter, whereas there is a slim possibility to be re-admitted as a divided China with dual representation. The basis for this proposal can be found in an examination of the policies established under the UN Charter. Paragraph 2, Article of the Charter reads:

> *The admission of any such state to membership in the United nations will be effected by a decision of the General Assembly upon the recommendation of the Security Council.*

According to the advisory opinion of the International Court of Justice (March 3, 1950) such recommendation by the Security Council is a legal perquisite. Paragraph 2, Article 18 of the Charter explicitly states: Admission of a new member to the United Nations is an "important question." Recommendation for admission of a new member should be made by an affirmative vote of nine members including the concurring votes of the permanent members as stated in Paragraph 3, Article 27. In other words, the permanent members of the Security Council can veto the admission of Taiwan as a new member even if nine members on the Council vote in favor of it.

Without doubt, Taiwan's application for membership to UN would be vetoed by the People's Republic of China in the Security Council. A white paper published by the People's Republic of China on "The Taiwan Question and the Reunification of China" in 1993 states:

Taiwan has belonged to China since ancient times. It was known as 'Yizhou' or 'Liuqui' in antiquity. Many historical records and annals documented the development of Taiwan by the Chinese people in earlier periods....This was the historical fact of how Taiwan, like other parts of China, came to be opened up and settled by the Chinese people of various nationalities. From the very beginning, Taiwan society derived from the source of the Chinese cultural tradition. This basic fact had not changed even during the half century of Japanese occupation

Moreover, when Nicaragua and eleven other members requested the inclusion on the agenda an item on the "consideration of the exceptional situation of the Republic of China in Taiwan in the international context" on June 28, 1994, Mr. Lee Zhaoxing, the PRC's permanent representative to the United Nations, responded to the Secretary-General in a letter of July 22, 1994 as follows (A/49/274):

Taiwan has belonged to China since ancient times. This is a historical fact that nobody can change. China's sovereignty over Taiwan was reaffirmed in the Cairo Declaration of 1943 and Potsdam Declaration of 1945. . .
The United Nations is an intergovernmental organization composed of sovereign states. Article 4 of the Charter of the United Nations stipulates in explicate terms that only sovereign states are entitled to membership in the United Nations. The principle of 'universality of membership' is only applicable to sovereign states. Taiwan, as a province of China, has no right whatsoever to be a member of the United Nations and, therefore, the principle of universality of membership does not apply in this case.

In view of the two above statements, the People's Republic of China would definitely veto Taiwan's bid to the United Nations as a new member.

In 1971, when the question of China's representation in the United Nations was discussed in the 26th session of the General Assembly, the United States and some other member states were in favor of dual representation for the Republic of China on Taiwan, whereby the ROC would keep its seat in the General Assembly. Albania and its allies objected. It suggested that if Taiwan wished to join the UN, it could apply for new membership, knowing full well that the People's republic of China would exercise its veto power in the Security council.

Veto Power Cannot Be Abolished

Some people have suggested that in the future, the veto in the Security Council might be abolished. Hardly. Based on historical facts upon which veto power was established, it is highly improbable. When the United Nations Conference on International Organization was held in San Francisco in 1945, many delegates opposed the veto power, but the four sponsor governments, i.e. China, the United States, the United Kingdom, and the Soviet Union were insistent upon preserving their authority to veto.

The tone of their statements clearly indicated a "no veto, no Charter" position. Veto power represents unanimous rule of the Great Powers, and they argued that it was consistent with political reality and a necessary condition for the creation of the organization. Furthermore, they believed that the organization would break down if enforcement action were undertaken against a permanently member. They also pointed out that even the five major powers could not act alone, since even under the unanimity requirement, any decision of the Security Council would have to include the concurring votes of at least two [now four] non-permanent members. stated otherwise, it would be possible for five [now seven] non-permanent members to exercise a "joint veto." Even without individual veto power, the non-permanent members have group veto power.

Eliminating the veto in the Security Council is made even more difficult when such a step requires an amendment to the UN Charter. Article 108 of the Charter stipulates that any amendment must be ratified by two-thirds of the members of the United Nations including all permanent members of the security Council. In other words, permanent members of the Security council have the right to veto any amendment to the Charter by not ratifying the amendment. Undoubtedly, the People's Republic of China would veto such an amendment by not ratifying it.   thus as long as the People's Republic of China is one of the permanent members of the Security Council, Taiwan will definitely have no chance to be admitted to the UN as a new member.

Dual Representation

Two options are available for the ROC on Taiwan to try to obtain re-admission to the UN, but again the problem is whether it can muster "sufficient votes" in the general Assembly. The first is to propose an amendment to Resolution 2758 (XXVI). When the "shoe was on the other foot" and Taiwan was on the inside occupying the UN seat for

China while the People's Republic was on the outside trying to gain admission, the General Assembly had previously voted seven times from 1961 to 1970 stating that the deprivation of the seat of the Republic of China was an important question, therefore requiring a two-thirds vote. When the General Assembly voted on this issue in 1971, it reversed itself leading to the adoption of resolution 2758 recognizing the People's republic of China as the only legitimate representative to the United Nations with the ouster of the Republic of China on Taiwan.

Resolution 2758 was able to muster a two-thirds favorable vote, (76 to 35 with 17 abstentions) though legally it could be adopted by a simple majority, because the important question proposal was rejected. So whether two-thirds or a simple majority can pass an amendment is still a controversial question. Some diplomats continue to insist that a two-third vote is needed, while others maintain a simple majority is sufficient. Since this is a legal question, the International Court of Justice could be requested to give an advisory opinion.

Second, the ROC on Taiwan can try to regain admission by asking friendly UN members to submit a draft resolution to the General Assembly stating that the People's Republic of China and the Republic of China on Taiwan are a divided country and have been ruled separately since 1949, and a divided nation can have dual representation. There is precedence for dual representation in the United nations. Witness East and West Germany before unification, north and South Korea, the 12 republics of the Soviet Union before its collapse, the four republics of the former Yugoslavia, as well as the Czech and Slovakia republics split in 1993 from Czechoslovakia. The adoption of the resolution needs a two-third vote.

No doubt, such a resolution to give Taiwan dual representation would provoke a challenge from the People's Republic of China to cll for the question to come before the Security Council rather than the General Assembly just as heretofore in all dual representation cases cited above. To overcome this challenge, a sentence can be added to the draft resolution thus: "Since the question of which government to represent a member to the UN is to be considered by the General Assembly [Resolution 396(v) of December 14, 1950], dual representation should also be considered by the General Assembly from now on."

What determines "sufficient votes?" Foreign Minister Frederick Chien called it the "magic number of votes" and his estimate is 123 votes. Actually the necessary votes could be fewer because according to Article 126 of the Rules of Procedure of the General Assembly, abstentions are not counted in calculating a majority or two-thirds vote and there are always some abstentions. If we assume that all 185 members of the United Nations General Assembly participated in voting and 10 percent abstained, only 84 votes would be needed for a simple majority and 111 votes would be needed for a two-thirds vote. If the number of abstentions is greater than 10 percent, then the "magic number of votes" would even be smaller.

At present, only 29 member states of the United Nations recognize the Republic of China on Taiwan. It is possible that members states who do not recognize Taiwan might vote for its admission to the United Nations. Yet in the General Debate of the General Assembly during the past two years, only 20 some members supported Taiwan in its bid for admission. This number is far too distant from the "magic number" of votes needed. Thus the task of the Taiwan government is a long and difficult one.

Over the last two years some friendly members to Taiwan in the United Nations proposed that the General Assembly establish a special committee to study the unique situation of the Republic of China on Taiwan. However, each year, the General Committee of the General Assembly decided not to recommend inclusion of this item on the agenda. Again, this shows how difficult it is for the Republic of China on Taiwan to be readmitted to the United Nations. Difficult it may be, but it is still not impossible.

It is worthy to note also that should a power struggle come about in the post-Deng Xiao Ping period, the victorious faction would be more likely to reconcile and cooperate with the ROC on Taiwan in order to obtain economic assistance to improve the Mainland's economy. That Taiwan is a province of China and that there is only one China is a firm conviction of the Chinese Communists, young and old, and they are not likely to favor a "One Taiwan, One China" policy.

Conclusion

In view of the above analysis, Taiwan's application for new membership to the United Nations is absolutely impossible because under the UN Charter, the People's Republic of China have the right to veto it. On the other hand, it is possible, though very difficult, for the Republic of China on Taiwan to regain a seat in the General Assembly as dual representation for China. Therefore the people of Taiwan must be realistic and find out what the related provisions of the Charter and resolutions are in order to act intelligently. In this manner, any effort to regain membership in the United Nations will not be in vain.

+++++

HEGEL

and CHINA'S POLITICAL FUTURE

by Vincent Chen, Ph.D.

Hegel's political philosophy contains lessons applicable to the political problems that will arise in China in the Twenty-First century.

Georg Wilhelm Friedrich Hegel (1770-1831 was a nineteenth-century German philosopher. He was a Suabian and the son of a government official. The region of Suabia has been the cradle of more thinkers and poets than any other part of Germany, and the area is known for a mystic strain of self-centered religiosity. Similarly, the people are known for the ability to combine spirituality with exceptional shrewdness and a practical business sense.

Hegel studied at the renowned theological seminary at Tubingen University, where he began an exploration of Immanuel Kant (1724-1804). His immersion in the study of Greek poetry and philosophy led him to the idea of a folk religion, far removed from formal theology and ritual. Instead, it was based on a people's ethics and natural laws. Thus, Hegel's Philosophy generally carries both religious and pragmatistic overtones.

The Spirit of the World

The foremost conception in Hegel's philosophical thought is the "spirit of the world." The spirit [as consciousness] can be viewed as a real, concrete and objective force. It can be identified as the essence of man and his history. It can be traced throughout the course of human history, as history can be seen as the unfolding of the spirit, or as the spirit becomes unified in its manifestation of history.

The German "spirit" is a masculine noun, conjuring the notion of a person actually and creatively at work, implying activism and subjectivism. Hegel extends subjectivism to extremes by proclaiming the most subjective to be actually the most objective. The spirit is a personalized entity, and the most objective entity at that, completely outside the self as well as inside it.

In English, this spirit may be translated in consciousness. The consciousness of things and the consciousness of self are the first two stages in the development of thought. The two are related in the same fashion as the objective and subjective. Only reason can bring them into unity and identity, thus consciousness of reason may be designated the third stage.

In Hegelian terms, reason is not a substance, but a subject, i.e., it is reason that becomes conscious of itself, or its spirit. The revelation of the spirit is the order of the world and its high stage the idea of God in the world. Even as the idea of God spreads throughout the world, it becomes the spirit of the world that creates all phenomena.

the idea of God is the representation of the divine absolute or religion which is perfected in the true knowledge of God. Here, there are three stages as well; reason, spirit and religion. For Hegel, philosophy, in its search for truth, is a dialectic process that creates different stages as it passes through them. Truth includes the negative which it negates. This negated aspect could be called an error. Each stage in the forward movement of the mind negates the preceding stage; it is built upon its antecedent. That which vanishes in the process must be looked upon as essential, yet not as something fixed and cut off from that which is true. Similarly, that which is true should not be looked upon as only positive, dead and static. This process of becoming and passing away truly exists and constitutes the actual reality and active life of truth. Hegelian conception of truth is always in flux, relativistic, dynamic and progressive.

In Judging this ongoing movement, Hegel says, the particular configuration of spirit and specific thoughts do not endure; however, they are necessary aspects, as they are negative and vanishing aspects. The essence, or truth, in the antecedent is preserved in the remaining movement, and in it the various spiritual configurations recall their antecedents and preserve what is true. What is being negated in the dialectic process is at once superseded and preserved. The works, supersede, carries the connotation of preserving what is replaced.

The key thought in Hegel's philosophy of history is that history reveals the gradual unfolding of the truth. In history, the dialectic of the spirit is explicitly working out its themes, and philosophy is one aspect of the general spirit at work in history. One must note that it is only one spirit, as the core or inner nexus, which expresses itself in various fields, such as law, ethics, religion, art, fashion, manners, commerce and industry. The spirit is only one, it is the substantive spirit of an epoch, of a nation, of a period that forms in many ways. In short, the spirit is the inevitable philosophical tide of the time that dominates or controls the development of all the fields of that time. And through the core or nexus, the various individual fields become linked together into a system commanded by the general conception known as the spirit.

Dialectic Idealism

It is necessary to further discuss and analyze dialectic idealism in order to illuminate the dynamic and developing nature of the idea of God and its manifestation --- the spirit of the world, as well as the harmony of god and man (天人合一). Dialectic, in Platonian terms, is the process of conversation. It can also be the process of discourse, dialogue, discussion or debate which, as a result of the clash of ideas, elicits truth and quashes error; finally reason irrationality emerges as the essence of the truth at that point. Hegel uses this dialectic logic as the philosophical method for analyzing the progress of history.

The dialectic method is nothing if separated from the contents or object under analysis. It is at work in the object and moves it along. The true logic is concerned with the ground of being, the beginning and end of philosophy. In short, it is ontology. Dialectics is thus descriptive, descriptive of the process of thought that one must experience in order to understand it. It shares something of the intuitive quality of direct experience.

The central experience with which dialectics struggles is the inadequacy of all concepts. Such concepts must be made to correspond to the fluidity and richness of life. Hegelian conception rather than concept is intended to be broader and more comprehensive. While it is fluid, there remains a persistent core.

The dialectic is the movement of conceptions, the dynamic process by which they are distilled. It is not static or fixed, but forever evolving and achieving new forms as relations with other conceptions change the perspectives, hoping to achieve a true reflection of reality.

The law of dialectics posits the thesis-antithesis-synthesis triad. In discourse where the movement of conceptions takes place, a thesis arouses an antithesis. A synthesis preserves as well as supersedes the combination of antecedent thesis and antithesis into one, with the elimination of errors in both thesis and antithesis. It is through such a synthesis that the conceptions reach ever high levels of truth. Then, the synthesis becomes a new thesis, and the process begins anew. This Hegelian dialectic process is a sound and objective description of what has actually occurred in history of the spirit as a general conception. Under the dictates of the spirit, the events in history forever progress in a dialectic manner. Without end, a new wave rises to overtake an old receding one.

The power of negation, of error, in the dialectic process is the originator of ever-new thought. Philosophical thought records and analyzes the experiences in history which have been made by the spirit. Hegelian dialectics is rooted in ontological (historical) and metaphysical (philosophic) assumptions. Apart from the ontological assumption which we have described, the metaphysical assumption is the core of Hegelain philosophy; the absolute is reason. Hegel asserts that dialectics can be god thinking himself in man or eternal reason realized in man's thought, hence the harmony of God and man. After the dialectic is considered, the truth emerges.

The idea of becoming is important to Hegel; all higher being is movement, development, action and history. Thus, God is also becoming. God as merely being is lifeless, an abstraction or motionless form. However, for Hegel, God is an active spiritual being, full of life and unfolding with respect to His inner nature. As so the spirit of the world is always progressing and developing. God is truly real, yet what is here and now in existence is part phenomenal and part real. The dialectic process distinguishes the real from the unreal and makes God's truth prevail over error. In this fashion, God continuously emanates His ideas for the attainment of His ultimate end---the absolute truth.

Hegel's Political Ideas

The Ethical State

Inheriting the notion of the ancient Greek city-state as a community, Hegel considers the state as an ethical entity. The state is empowered to make and enforce laws to actualize ethical ideas in society, in order that individuals may live a virtuous life. Since the state, like the church, is the actual reality of ethical ideas, both seek the same goal: God. Their separation is akin to specialization of function. While the state is charged with realizing conscious religion or self-conscious rationality in philosophy, the church concentrates on providing a community in which man may become certain of God. Yet, the salvation of man is the concern of both state and church.

Law and Constitution

Ethical ideas not only guide the conduct of individuals but also limit the power of government. Suabia is the southwestern corner of Germany, where the constitutional tradition of government by consent is firmly entrenched. This experience testifies to Hegel's postulation that the citizens must effectively participate in lawmaking in an ethical community. In his study of the German constitution and his work on natural law and ethics, Hegel emphasis the importance of the government of law, not of man. It follows that the power of government is limited by ethics or natural law because the constitution, as basic law, is an embodiment of ethical ideas that define the mutual rights and duties of the state and its citizens. In fact, many German state constitutions are based on customary law. Custom is second nature, so natural law is upheld. Hegel's belief in constitutional or limited government is apparent, even though he favors authoritarianism for national security and for the realization of ethical ideas.

Freedom

To Hegel, individuals have an ethical being insofar as they belong to the ethical community which is the state. Only in the state where ethical ideas prevail, can individuals enjoy genuine freedom; for the state is the actual reality of ethical ideas. It is the duty of the individual to be a member of the state. This does not entail the totalitarian destruction of the individual, rather, an insistence that it is the duty of individuals to realize ethical ideas by freely participating in the community. for those who would insist that the state be an institution that issues commands or exercises despotic power in a totalitarian fashion, such a position may be considered destructive of the state's essential characteristic, and this subversive. Hence, a denial of the state's true concern with the just and ethical, a denial of the state as based upon law.

In Hegel's view, the Magna Carta, the Bill of Rights and the positive enactment's in the British Constitution are the basic law that limits the power of government and keeps it within the sphere of ethical ideas. In modern terms, this may imply that the power of government should be under the control of natural law or the law of human rights. Otherwise, the government is one of tyranny, which has encroached upon the rights of people. Consequently, it loses its legitimacy of governing.

Under the influence of the French Revolution, freedom remains a central value in Hegel's philosophy. After repeated interpretation, he concluded that freedom is the activation of one's own tendency; it is the unfolding of oneself; it is self-realization. Contrary to the ordinary sense of freedom of will, Hegelian true freedom is the necessity of removing obstacles to freedom. As the root of human creativity, freedom is true inner law and true substance. As man is intended to be free as man, freedom is involved in the very idea of man. This metaphysical conception of meaningful destiny through self-fulfillment is vital to an understanding of Hegelian philosophy as it pertains to right, law and history. No government can abridge man of his freedom.

Condemnation of Revolution

Hegel is a conservative in the sense that he believes the community is an ever-growing entity. In the process of its growth, it dialectically preserves that which is real and true and removes that which is unreal and erroneous. Thus, dialectics sounds like a self-correction mechanism.

A new period naturally superseded the old, making the community even better. Thus Hegel prefers reforms to revolution. He asserts, "What is rational, that is actual and real; and what is actually real, that is rational." This proposition implies that there is the real and rational in actual existence, which is entitled to be preserved; this is a formula of quietism that provides the philosophical ground for peaceful reform. Of course, Hegel tells us that norms are indeed valid when they are directed toward changing that which is unreal and contingent. Yet, they are empty abstractions when they seek to change that which is actual and real as manifested by the spirit and God's idea. he vehemently opposes revolution, because it more often than not destroys what is real and unreal altogether in one sweeping measure, seriously damaging the cultural roots of a nation. Once violence has been taken up, it inevitably tends to become unlimited and excessive, resulting in immeasurable human suffering and sacrifice, let along enormous material losses. No wonder Hegel joined other great conservatives in condemning the excesses of the French Revolution.

Democracy

Hegel is also a liberal. The alternative to revolution is the peaceful evolution that democracy provides. In Germany, Hegel inherits the constitutional tradition of government of law and by consent. Though he turned against the French Revolution, he nonetheless became the philosopher of French revolutionary goals: freedom and a democracy where the citizen is the active participant. He was particularly impressed by English participatory democracy, where a representative government operated, with civil rights securely protected in the constitution.

He synthesized the best traditions of democracy in these three countries to form his own conception of democracy; a representative government in a participatory democracy, based on an ethics-oriented constitution. While he praised the Prussian state, with an authoritarian government, he predicted that there would soon be a popular representative government for all of Germany.

Essentially, Hegel's conception of democracy is built on his metaphysical conception of freedom. Here we may presume that freedom requires free speech, free assembly, free association, free debate and free election, as the necessary paraphernalia of the representative government Hegel envisioned. A free press and a free political opposition would perform the function of purifying society and government. free debate and periodic free elections would facilitate the conflict of ideas with majority rule as procedural justice for resolution. this would enable the new, true ideas to replace old, erroneous ideas and policies. consequently, society continues the march of progress. Basically, democracy is a process of dialectics in which the idea of God and concomitant spirit of the world realizes itself.

Liberal democracy is the Western tradition rooted in ancient Athens and the Roman Republic. Its modern form since the Industrial Revolution has operated for two hundred years. In this period, democracy has promoted and insured freedom, peace, justice and prosperity for the Western world. This long political experiment has proven that democracy is a successful political system, even as other competing systems have fallen one after another.

Then what is China's choice for its political future? Democracy. Hegel thought it ridiculous to suggest that people, including the Chinese, are not mature enough for a participatory democracy. The present Communist totalitarianism in China would inevitably collapse, sooner or later, because it violates Hegel's philosophical logic and runs counter to the democratic tide of the times that is the spirit of the world and the unfolding idea of God.

+++++

WHITHER CHINA;

DIVISION OR UNIFICATION?

Comments on the relations between the two sides of the Formosa Strait

by Charles C. M. Chung

The results of the U.S. review of it Taiwan policy has finally been made public. It seems that both sides of the Formosa Strait have gained some benefit from the first U.S. policy review in the last fifteen years. In particular, the U.S. has agreed to change the name of The Coordination Council of North America Affairs.......to: **The Taipei Economic and Cultural Representative Office in the United States.** The inclusion of the name "Taipei" implies that the U.S. recognized Taiwan as a political entity in a divided China, although the U.S. Government still insists on a "one China policy" and declares that it cannot support Taiwan's admission to the United Nations nor to any international organization in which only sovereign states can be members. This being the case, would it be better for both sides of the Formosa Strait to continue the present *de facto* division or rather to seek some form of temporary union without prejudice to any future agreement on complete unification?

Difficulties in Achieving Unification

Both sides of the Formosa Strait insist that "there is only one China" and advocate the unification of China. But Communist China maintains that this "one China" is the People's Republic of China; and the Republic of China on Taiwan, on the other hand, asserts that this "one China" is the Republic of China which came into being in 1911 and continues to exist in Taiwan today and that the People's Republic of China does not equate "China."

On the matter of unification, Communist China claims that the Central People's Government of the People's Republic of China is the only legitimate government of China and Taiwan is an inseparable part of China, (Section one, PRC 1993 white paper) and that the Communist Government is the Central Government and the Taiwan government is only a local government. Jian Zemin told Chang Chien-Pang, a former high official from Taiwan, that "if Taiwan is also admitted to the United nations, would it not become that there are two central governments in one country? If there is a separation in the national territory, the separatist local government can only negotiate with the central government to resolve their dispute, and should not declare itself as another central government; otherwise, our country would become really divided." On the other hand, the Republic of China in Taiwan maintains that although both Mainland China and Taiwan are parts of Chinese territory, they are political enties of equal status, since China is in a temporary state of division, and each government controls one side of the Strait (Program of National Unification). It is therefore evident that the two governments on the opposite sides of the Strait hold completely different views on "one China" and unification of China."

While The Republic of China on Taiwan is making every effort to gain re-admission to the United Nations, Communist China maintains that after the restoration of all the legitimate rights of the People's Republic of China in the United nations in 1971, the question of so-called Chinese representation in the United Nations organization has been completely settled, and therefor there can be no such question as Taiwan's re-admission to the United Nations (Section 5, PRC's 1993 white paper). Thus, Communist China is unalterably opposed to the re-admission of the republic of China on Taiwan to the United nations. It insists that negotiations on unification should come first. However, Taiwan wants its re-admission to the United Nations first and negotiations for the unification of China to come later. This clearly shows that the divided rule on the two sides of the Strait will continue and it would be impossible to achieve unification of china if both sides do not change their position and do not want to have direct contact.

Cases of Division and Unification

Countries which separate and then unite or which are united and then become separated are common historical phenomena since ancient times. There are numerous actual cases of members of the united nations which have gone through division and unification or vice versa. In addition to East and West Germany, there are Egypt and Syria. These two countries were original members of the United nations since October 24. 1945, but they were joined to form the United Arab republic as a result of a plebiscite held on February 21, 1958 and thus became a single member of the United Nations. Syria restored its independence on October 13, 1961 as well as its own membership in the United Nations.

The federation of Malaya was admitted to the United nations on September 17, 1957 and then joined Singapore, Sabah (North Borneo) and Sarawak to form a new federation. On September 16, 1963, the name of the Federation of Malaya was consequently changed to Malaysia.

Singapore became independent on August 9, 1965 and was admitted to the United nations on September 21 in the same year.

Tanganyika and Zanzibar were admitted to the United nations on December 14, 1961 and December 16, 1963 respectively, and then became a single member of the United Nations after the Articles of Union between them was ratified on April 26, 1964 and formed the United republic of Tanganyika and Zanzibar. This name was changed to the United Republic of Tanzania on November 1, 1964.

Yemen and Democratic Yemen were admitted to the United nations on September 13, 1947 and September 14, 1967 respectively. They were merged to become a single member of the United Nations under the name of "Yemen" on May 22, 1990.

Czechoslovakia was an original member of the United Nations since October 24, 1945. In a letter dated December 10, 1992, its permanent representative informed the Secretary-General that the Czeck and Slovak Federal Republic would cease to exist on December 31, 1992, and that the Czech republic and the Slovak Republic, as successor states, would apply for membership in the United nations separately. As a result, they were approved to become separate members of the United nations on January 19, 1993.

It is possible that South Korea and North Korea might be unified some day in the future. Similarly, no one can say that the Czech Republic and the Slovak Republic might not be unified as one country again. Thus, division today....may be unification tomorrow.

One may also look at the Soviet union which is not only an original member of the United nations, but also a permanent member of the Security Council. When former president Gorbachev sensed that the old Soviet system was going to fail, he adopted three reform measure to remedy the situation: Glasnost, Democratization and Perestroika. He soon realized that these measures would not help, but he did not resort to force to maintain the unified Soviet system, and was courageous enough to allow member Republics of the Soviet Union to secede and become independent. People all over the world admired him and praised him as "a hero whether he is successful or not." In addition to Byelorussia (now Belarus) and Ukraine, twelve member republics of the former Soviet union have become independent and are all admitted to the United nations. No matter what other benefits may accrue to its people as a result of this dissolution, the former Soviet union has increased its membership in the United nations from three to twelve, making a total of fifteen. This may be what Stalin had dreamed of, but was not able to achieve.

Yugoslavia is another example. In accordance with the recommendations contained in the Security Council resolution of September 19, 1992, the General Assembly decided on September 22, 1992 that the Federal Republic of Yugoslavia (Serbia and Montenegro) could not automatically take over the United nations membership of the former Socialist Federal Republic of Yugoslavia, and that it must apply for its own membership, and should not participate in the work of General Assembly (United Nations document A/RES/47/1). The Security Council further adopted a resolution on April 28, 1993 which did not permit the Federal Republic of Yugoslavia to participate in the work of Summer Session of the Economic and Social Council in that year (A/RES/1993). Of the six member Republics of the Socialist Federal Republic of Yugoslavia, four were admitted to the United nations in 1992 and 1993; Bosnia and Herzegovina; Croatia; the former Yugoslav Republic of Macedonia; and Slovenia.

The problems which confront the United Nations after the end of cold war are not those of international aggression, but are those of ethnic conflicts and civil wars. The United nations has been criticized that in his haste to admit twelve member republics of the former Soviet union and the four member republics of the former Yugoslavia, it had ignored the traditional criteria for recognizing new states, which includes the determination whether a state is in fact in existence and whether the applicant is a qualified political and social entity. Under certain circumstances, such hasty admission could involve the United Nations in dangerous and costly ethnic and territorial conflicts. But there is a trend for ethnic groups to gain independence. In the interest of "Universality" of its membership, the United Nations is obliged to admit them.

The best way to achieve some form of unification is direct negotiation between the two sides of the strait. Taiwan may offer mainland some kind of economic assistance to develop its economy, and mainland China could agree to the Republic of China on Taiwan joining the United nations as a member of the General Assembly under an appropriate name following the precedent of the former Soviet union which held three seats in the United nations before its dissolution.

Mainland China needs Taiwan's capital and technology, and Taiwan needs Mainland's cheap labor and raw material as well as market. So, this is the right time for both sides to help each other for their mutual benefit, thus achieving some form of unification in the spirit of accommodation and cooperation which prevails after the "cold war." In this way, China would have two votes in the United Nations instead of only one. If both sides can cooperate with each other in earnest, people on both sides of the Strait will benefit greatly. This surely is a sensible way to deal with the current situation.

Moreover, this writer also believes that one way to deal with Tibet's independence movement could be to allow Tibet, as an autonomous entity, to apply for membership in the United nations General Assembly, thus enabling China to have three seats in the united nations. At the same time, a **People's Union of China** consisting of three parts of China could be established in Beijing. Each part would send a delegate to the **Union** to formulate measures for all parts to cooperate with and to assist each other, and to discuss what position they should take in common in the United nations. The current trend is for ethnic groups to obtain independence. This is why several members of the United nations have their territory divided into two or more states and apply for multiple united nations memberships. There, it would be politic to allow Tibet to acquire its own status in the United nations so that some form of unification could be achieved for all of China.

In the event that the above-mentioned union is established, each of the three members should neither try to gain benefits only for itself, not try to preserve its own political power or the personal position of certain individuals, but should subject its own interests to the common interests of the **Union** as a whole in order to make the Chinese nation both unified and strong. If the three members could all do their best for the Union, then the true re-unification of a greater China could, in the not too distant future, become a reality.

Conclusions

There are several prerequisites for the **People's Union of China** to succeed. For Mainland China, it should take an enlightened attitude in dealing with it's smaller counterparts, and treat Taiwan as an equal political entity. It should at the same time, carry out political reforms and relinquish the concept of "one party rule". national sovereignty belongs to people as a whole, but not to any political party or any individual person. Whether a political party or an individual person should hold political power or should continue to hold such power must be decided by the people. On the other hand, Taiwan should desist from any efforts aiming at independence. Taiwan is a part of China. If China remains divided, it would certainly not serve the best interests of the Chinese people both on the Mainland and on Taiwan. In the meantime, Taiwan would help the situation if it is willing to amend its "Guidelines for National unification" to permit earlier direct official negotiation with the Chinese Communist Government.

People both on Taiwan and on the Mainland as well as overseas Chinese share the same wish that both sides of the Formosa Strait reach some form of accommodation. This is also the wish of other peoples and political leaders throughout the world. it is now high time for China to progress from a state of division to some acceptable form of unification. This writer sincerely hopes that political leaders on both sides of the Strait would give serious consideration to this idea, and take positive steps towards its realization.

+++++

PROBLEMS OF HUMAN RIGHTS

IN THE REPUBLIC OF CHINA

by Victor T. H. Tsuan Ph.D.

Generally speaking, the concept of human rights means that all individuals everywhere are entitled to life, liberty and pursuit of happiness on this earth, regardless of race, sex, language, or religion.

In China the promotion of human dignity and mutual respect for human rights was well developed in the Confucian classics. Confucius [551-479 B.C.] has generally been recognized as the founder of Chinese humanism. His philosophy is humanistic, dealing chiefly with human relations and virtues, such as people living in harmony with each, encouraging a sense of justice and fairness, and building a spirit of tolerance and willingness to compromise.

The classics of **"Book of History"** and **"Book of Poetry"** contain elaborate statements regarding the theoretical conception of government. Confucius said:

"A ruler rules by the authority of the mandate of Heaven, which is readily transferred to another, once the incumbent becomes unworthy of the trust."

Heaven is an ancient Chinese term for deity and was understood by Confucius to be a cosmic spiritual moral power similar to the concept of natural law in Western philosophy. A citizen's right of dissent was not recognized in the West until the end of the seventeenth century when John Locke brought up the subject in his famous book, "Two Treatises of Government," more than two thousand years after Confucius' original statement on this matter.

In the West, the Stoic School founded by Zeno in 308 B.C. in Athens also proposed numerous human rights. But they disappeared during the Medieval Age, since the Judeo-Christian tradition rejected the notion that people had a right to earthly happiness, and their common belief in the divine right of kings. However, human rights reappeared in the eighteenth century under the influence of Locke and a group of French philosophers like Voltaire, Rousseau and Montesquieu who strongly advocated basic human rights. This was followed by two basic human rights documents: The Declaration of Independence in the United States in 1776, and The Declaration of the Rights of Man in France in 1789.

Prior to 1945 there was by and large, universal acceptance of the view that how a state treated its citizens was mainly its own concern. The individual alone, or collectively, was considered merely as an object, not as a subject of international law. There was no limit to the power a given state might exercise to impose its will on the people under its jurisdiction. Traditionally, only the individual's state could sue in an international court, or protest through diplomatic channels. It was not a question of the protection of human rights, but rather the injury to a national was deemed as an injury to his state. Hence it was the state, not the individual that enjoyed the right of protection. The individual injured by his own state was without recourse because no other state could presume to press his claim. Under the United nations, however, the Declaration of Human Rights was adopted in 1948, which broaden the scope of what constituted violations of human rights, especially with respect to the individual.

In the United States, legal basis for human rights is found in the first ten amendments of the constitution. Prior to World War I there were two separate systems of human rights and fundamental freedoms in America; federal protection extended only to a limited number of cases in the areas of treason, sedition, and citizenship. State Constitutions and statutes provided other protection. the process of merging these provisions into a single national system was first made popular by President Woodrow Wilson, and later expanded by President Franklin Delano Roosevelt. Since then, the American people have successfully solved most of their human rights problems.

In the republic of China, the basic human rights and fundamental freedoms are protected by Chapter two of the Constitution. Article seven states: *"All citizens of the Republic of China irrespective of sex, religion, race, class, or party affiliation, shall be equal before the law."*

Freedom of residence, speech, teaching, writing, publication, privacy of correspondence, religious belief, assembly and association, choosing a vocation property, presenting petitions, lodging complaints, instituting legal proceedings, election, recall, initiative, referendum, taking public examination, and holding public office are all guaranteed by the Constitution.

In 1975 J. Terry Emerson, a legal consultant of the U.S. Senate, wrote a report which on February 18, 1975 Senator Barry Goldwater read on the Senate floor, which states in part:
"The human rights which I found to be healthy and alive in the Republic of China, but which are without any question denied by the Communist regime on the Mainland, include:
1. *The right of free travel and movement inside the country and abroad.*
2. *The right of seeking job opportunities according to one's own talents, not at the direction of the central government.*
3. *The right of free exercise of religious and ethical devotion.*
4. *The right to vote in truly free elections and to run for elective office.*

5. *The right of independent newspapers and magazines to exist.*
6. *The right of free expression.*
7. *The right to enjoy a free and wide ranging education designed to create independent thinking and knowledgeable citizens.*
8. *The freedom to respect and preserve the Chinese cultural heritage, without ridicule or punishment.*
9. *The right of free emigration*
10. *The right of private ownership and investment of property.*
11. *A free judiciary.*
12. *Freedom from aggression.*

In fact, the Constitution of the Republic of China coves more protection of human rights and fundamental freedoms than the first ten amendments of the Constitution of the united States of America, even though the U.S. Supreme Court decisions have covered a wide range of cases, such as equal treatment of racial groups, alien expulsion or deportation, arrests, search, seizure, freedom of speech and of the press, religious freedom, double jeopardy, child labor, free trial, women's suffrage, etc. Several other human rights and fundamental freedoms such as the right to candidacy and governmental actions against racial discrimination are still insufficiently protected under the legal system of the united States of America.

Over the last fifty years the United Nations has been responsible for a steady growth of international law and institutions designed to articulate and protect human rights. The Charter itself lists the promotion of human rights among the major purposes of the organization. The Universal Declaration of Human Rights promulgated by the General Assembly of the United Nations in December 1948 spells out a whole series of international instruments for the promotion of various human rights. Several of these including Conventions on the Prevention and Punishment of the Crime of Genocide, on the Elimination of All Forms of Racial Discrimination, on Economic, social, and Cultural Rights, on civil and Political Rights, have obtained a sufficient number of ratification or accessions to enter into force as treaties binding upon their signatories. Nevertheless, the burden of implementation has, with few exceptions, been left to the individual states themselves, and progress in developing effective international protective techniques has been a major task for the Human Rights Commission of the United Nation's Economic and Social Council.

All kinds of human rights were asserted in response to certain particular problems of the time, and in order to understand any particular human right in question requires that one is aware of what these problems really are. Since 1949, the republic of China in Taiwan has accelerated social and economic progress and established a stable and just social order, so that every citizen can achieve complete fulfillment of his or her aspirations and live a life of prosperity unprecedented in Chinese history. It has also narrowed the gap between the rich and poor. Taiwan is a beacon of human rights and fundamental freedoms, a military fortress, a custodian of Chinese culture, a center of learning and one of the world's great tourist attractions.

The occasional debate on the issue of human rights in Taiwan has generated more heat than light because it has failed to recognize its historical context. How can anyone understand the composition of the British House of Lords if one is not conscious of its historical continuity from the time of landed power in feudal society? Aside from the occasional false accusations of human rights violations in the republic of China by a few dissenters or liberal news reporters, both the United nations' Human rights Commission and Amnesty International have disclosed that human rights and fundamental freedoms are sufficiently protected by the government of the Republic of China.

+++++

"t'ien hsia wei kung"

[The world belongs to all]

Chapter III

SINO-AMERICAN RELATIONS

CHINESE - AMERICAN COOPERATION

IN PROMOTING

CHINA'S AGRICULTURAL EXTENSION

by Marguerite Atterbury, Ph.D.

The first objective of this research was to review in part the record of Chinese-American co-operation in promoting China's Agricultural Extension, as little-known period of history. Only a fraction of the available material could be utilized in the given space. But the workers whose vision showed the way to a better life for rural people have had so little publicity that even such a limited treatment might be useful.

The historical records of China have shown how from early times the rulers of the Middle Kingdom have stressed agricultural welfare. Chinese-American co-operation has introduced scientific techniques into this venerable culture-pattern, and has helped to create Agricultural Extension services which promoted rural welfare in China, and are now being welcomed in other Asian countries.

The second objective was to see if Chinese-American co-operation had made an "effective" contribution to the improvement of China's rural life, and to the development of a National Agricultural Extension System. the general categories of Extension and of allied activities favorable to the development of Extension, listed as follows:

1.   Provided trained leadership in the improvement of China's rural life, in agricultural education and research, in the organization and administration of a National Agricultural Extension System, in beneficial agricultural legislation, and in the solution of tenancy and land distribution problems.

2.   Taught scientific crop-improvement, animal husbandry, disease prevention and insect control for plants and animals; use of fertilizers and improved farm tools; and other up-to-date practices that could be added to China's age-old agricultural skills.

3.   **Taught better rural health practices and home management, including sanitation, child care and birth-control.**

4.   **Through modern engineering, promoted flood control, soil conservation and reclamation, irrigation, forestry, hydro-electric power, and improved communications.**

5.   **Promoted constructive organizations such as Co-operatives, farmers' associations, youth groups, family welfare clubs, popular education classes, etc..**

6.   **Improved rural economics through better practices in marketing, warehousing, the distribution of low-interest credit, and in village industries.**

7.   **Strengthened the ideals of Democracy, whereby human beings are considered valuable ends in themselves, to be accorded freedom in government,   self-expression, and in personality development.**

These categories cover main types of Extension, and allied activities favorable to Extension development. The cooperation between China and America was of two kinds: First, the cooperation with the rural population in China, and
Second, cooperation in training China's Agricultural Extension personnel in America. Every type of service listed above has been supplied to a certain extent through Chinese-American cooperation, though some services were emphasized more than others.

The samples given of training China's Agricultural Extension personnel in America indicate that the potential leaders have been encouraged to think of Agricultural Extension in relation to the rural needs, rather than merely as an academic subject to be taught in an educational institution.

A chart showing the categories of Extension and allied activities favorable to Extension development is given in Appendix D, pages 376-377, with some of the Extension services supplied by Chinese-American co-operation listed under each category. [NOTE; ABOVE CHART NOT FURNISHED WITH THIS MANUSCRIPT.]

Even in this very limited treatment, the contribution made by Chinese-American co-operation to the improvement of China's rural life, and to the development of A National Agricultural Extension System might be considered "effective." By 1946, according to "Agricultural Extension In China," The report of the National Agricultural Extension Commission of China, in Appendix B. the Commission had six divisions of Extension in its central Nanking headquarters, and had 351 "hsien" Extension officer is 14 Provinces. When this work was interrupted by *force majeure* of Communist attack, as it had been previously disrupted by the Sino-Japanese War, Chinese-American co-Operation was just developing an equivalent national Commission of Agricultural

Extension in the form of the Joint Commission of Rural Reconstruction, which proved useful when the Government of the Republic of China was transferred to Taiwan.

One Extension service too little emphasized in China has been Home Economics. Dr. P.W. Tsou, in his "Proposed Program of Agricultural Development in China," does not even list Home Economics as an important phase of Agricultural Extension. A beginning had been made, but not enough recognition had been given to the contribution that women could make to the improved family standard of living.

Another lack has been in teaching birth control through rural Extension service. The Mass Education Movement at Ting Hsien pioneered in using its district health stations to disseminate information on birth control, but other service organizations did not sufficiently follow this example.

The third objective was to see if Chinese-American co-0peration in China's Agricultural Extension has produced multi-national co-operation, especially in United Nations' Agencies, and to deduce principles for Technical Assistance Programs, especially those of Agricultural Extension under the Food and Agriculture Organization. The case studies have shown that many of the experts in Chinese-American co-operation have been recruited for multi-national co-operation. The chart on page 378, Appendix D, lists twelve who have gone into international service from their training period in China. [NOTE; NOT SUPPLIED WITH THE MANUSCRIPT.] [Publisher]

Many more could be enumerated. The case studies themselves showed international groups functioning for a common goal. Chinese-American co-operation is thus seen to have been a factor of synergism promoting symbiosis on a wider scale, and not a divisive policy for a bloc against the rest of the world.

As for deducing principles applicable to Technical Assistance Programs elsewhere, many of the activities related in the case studies have been incorporated in the world-wide programs of the Food and Agriculture Organization of the United Nations, which is really an over-all directing Extension Agency on the fourth, or international level. (Within each country having an Agricultural Extension Service, the organization usually operates on the three domestic levels of federal, state, and county.) The Technical Assistance Projects listed on page 379, Appendix D. from The Work of FAO, 1950/51: Report of the Director-General are practically all of a type previously tested in Chinese-American co-operation. [ABOVE MATERIAL NOT FURNISHED; publisher]

The general principles of Extension as observed at the Nanking college of Agriculture and Forestry have much in common with the recommendations in Measures for the Economic Development of Under-Developed Countries as reported by a group of experts appointed by the Secretary-General of the United Nations. Point Four and Education, a study by the Educational Policies Commission also has policies which are in harmony with the procedures found successful in Chinese-American co-operation.

The diagram on page 381 [NOT PROVIDED; publisher] indicates what simple services can greatly increase the income of many Asian farmers. The skills of the farmer's wife can raise the standard of living still further. The primary need seems to be not more research, but the practical application of the techniques already successfully demonstrated.

It is a sad commentary on human nature that "antagonism" is a much more familiar expression than its' antonym, "synergism."

This is a Big Game---not the World Series---but the adventure of ridding the earth of its' plagues, and multiplying its' friendly assets. It is hoped that as world ecology becomes better adjusted, symbiosis will be the rule instead of so often the exception. Perhaps, as the principles of synergism become widely demonstrated, especially through the agencies of the United Nations, all people may be drawn into making with world a real Home for the Human Race.

+++++

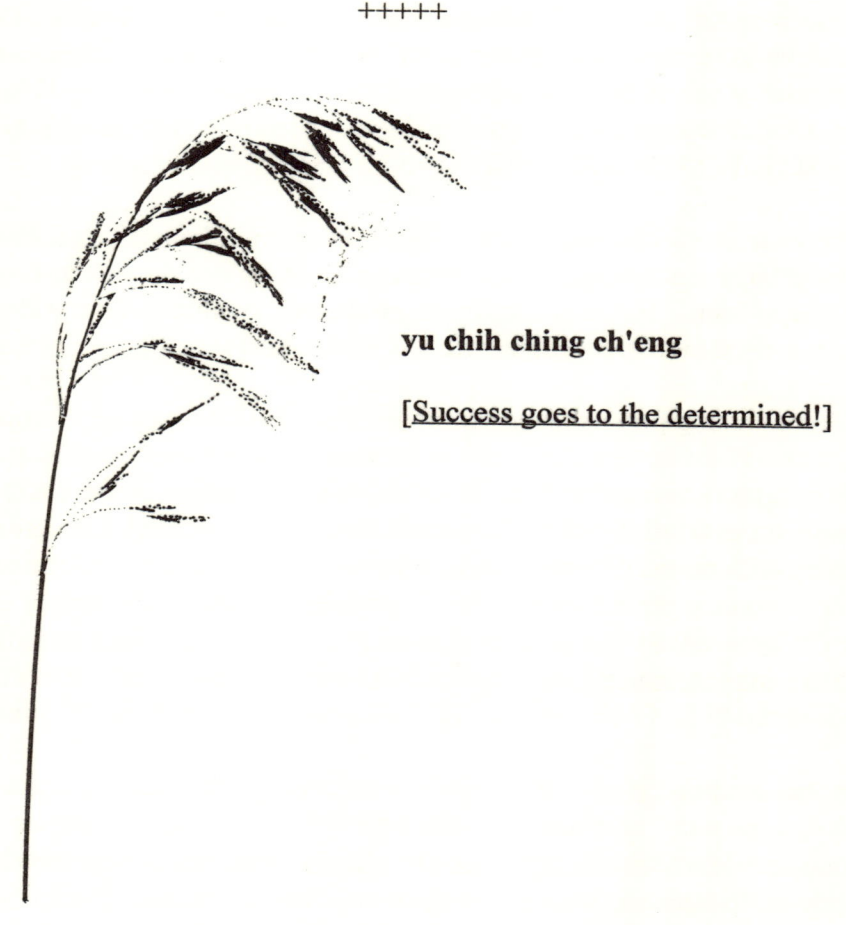

yu chih ching ch'eng

[Success goes to the determined!]

RONALD REAGAN

and the

UNITED STATES COMMITMENT TO TAIWAN

Anthony Kubek, Ph.D.

Ronald Reagan has long been associated with the cause of Taiwan, the Island-Republic of 21 million people off the coast of China. When Mao Tse-tung and the Communists took over mainland China in 1949, more than 1 million Nationalist leaders retreated to Taiwan including President Chiang Kai-shek who laid the groundwork for enormous progress in the Island-Republic.

As a two-term Governor of California, Ronald Reagan had for a number of years supported the Republic of China, and according to most public opinion polls at the time, so did most Americans. While Henry Kissinger accepted much credit for the success of Richard Nixon's administration, Reagan always believed that Richard Nixon was a foreign policy master, the one with a strategic view of the world. In the early 1970's President Nixon, contrary to what had been expected of Republicans for two decades, forged a friendly relationship with communist China. Yet no one admired Nixon more than Ronald Reagan. Reagan may be one of the last figures in America to have defended Nixon during the stormy days of "Watergate." In October 1971, because of Reagan's strong support of the Republic of China, Nixon sent him to Taipei to "do the dirty work of explaining Nixon's shift in China policy" to President Chiang Kai-shek on Taiwan.. At the same time, Secretary of State Henry Kissinger was in Peking secretly making a deal to recognize Communist China and cut back on U.S. ties to the Nationalist Chinese government.

One cannot imagine an assignment less appealing to a man with Reagan's convictions. But he went, and when he arrived at the summer Palace he was met by the Generalissimo and Madame Chiang. The old warrior was like a stone, looking straight ahead, silently, as Reagan explained why the move was one that the United States felt it had to make. Finally, Reagan rose and said, "I'm not happy about this and I know you're not happy. But it was going to happen in our lifetime, and it is better to have it happen under President Richard Nixon than under Hubert Humphrey."

The argument was that the opening to China would harm and distract the Soviet Russians. And if Humphrey, the liberal, had been elected president he might have abandoned Taiwan entirely, whereas under President Nixon we would still maintain relations, cultural if not diplomatic. If a Democrat had been making Nixon's trip to China, Reagan said in 1972, "I'd be up on the wall screaming because....a Democrat President would be appeasement-minded," but Nixon "only intends to establish communication."

On Nixon's return from his meeting with Mao Tse-tung in February, 1972, Reagan said he had asked him what would happen if Red China tried to take Taiwan by force. Nixon replied, "This country will protect and defend Taiwan."

In late 1977, the public relations firm of Michael Deaver and Peter Hannaford, which was handling governor Reagan's radio broadcasts, was invited to work for the Taiwan government. They asked Reagan if he had any objections. The governor, with hesitating, said: "We should accept." After discussing Taiwan, Reagan laughed: "I was the one selling them on Taiwan." He was outraged when President Carter established diplomatic relations with Communist China and abrogated the U.S. defense treaty with Taiwan. He complained it was "based on betrayal of the free Chinese on Taiwan. As a result the nations of the world have seen us cold-bloodedly betray a friend for political expediency."

In April 1978, governor Reagan made a trip to Asia. After visiting Japan during the first leg of the trip, he was interested in returning to Taiwan, where he had accepted an invitation to address the Chinese National Association of Industry and Commerce. It was during the rush hour in Taipei when he arrived and the Republic of China greeted Ronald Reagan as a good friend, virtually a hero. A large motorcade with R.O.C. and U.S. flags flying from the fenders of the autos made its' way through crowded downtown Taipei. People on both sides of the street waved and cheered Reagan, who was the most important American public figure to visit Taiwan since vice-president Nelson Rockefeller attended Chiang Kai-shek's funeral in 1975.

After attending an evening formal and many-course Chinese banquet hosted by Acting President C.K. Yen and, the next morning, a private breakfast with Chiang Ching-kuo, son of Chiang Kai-shek who would be taking office soon as President elect, the entourage went to Reagan's featured speaking engagement with members of the Chinese national Association of Commerce and Industry at a downtown hotel ballroom. He started his address detailing the economic accomplishments of the Republic of China and moving to the subject of U.S. - R.O.C. friendship. He said:

> "Vivid evidence that our friendship is a two-way street was given early this year when you sent a special trade mission to the U.S. for the express purpose of buying more than one-quarter of a billion dollars of American goods in order to reduce your trade surplus with us....Here we have evidence of each nation helping

the other. First, American aid at a time when you were embarking on modern-ization and industrialization of Taiwan in order to improve the lot of your people. Now, you are making a special effort to "buy American" at a time when we have a serious trade deficit.

This friendship and mutual trust goes back a long way. Our ties are strong. They bind us, but could they be broken? I am afraid that the answer is 'Yes,' they could under certain circumstances. But should they be broken and must they be broken? The answer in both cases is "NO," of course not."

Finally, Reagan made this perceptive observation: "If, in order to 'normalize' relations with Peking, the United States were to accede to its' three demands---breaking diplomatic relations with the Republic of China---breaking our mutual defense treaty of 1954 and withdrawing our remaining military advisors---then Peking could indeed argue with logic, that Taiwan and thus all of its' people had **become an internal matter and no longer any of America's business."** (Emphasis added.) As events eventually occurred since the U.S. recognition of the People's Republic of China (PRC) on January 1, 1979, the PRC constantly complained that any U.S. aid to Taiwan was an interference in China's internal affairs and should cease.

In terms of area and population, Taiwan is like a Biblical "David" arrayed against the mainland "Goliath." David needed his slingshot, and supply of ammunition and so does Taiwan. But even a spear or slingshot are objectionable items to the Chinese Communists. Therefore, no one should be surprised when Peking raised a terrific clamor about selling Taiwan a few fighter planes. The main U.S. reason for continuing arms sales was the refusal of the PRC to commit itself to peaceful resolution of the Taiwan issue. The PRC realized that unless it made certain concessions, it was not possible to undercut U.S. arms sales to Taiwan.

In various speeches, Governor Reagan boldly criticized the crude, shoddy treatment of the Republic of China by the Carter administration. At two a.m. in Taipei, only a few hours before President Carter made his dramatic recognition announcement, U.S. diplomats requested that President Chiang Ching-kuo be awakened to be told by American Ambassador Leonard Unger of the forthcoming "normalization"---a notice of scarcely seven hours before the American President went on the air with what he must regard as a master diplomatic stroke, Chiang, the son of the late President Chiang Kai-shek was deeply shocked. His immediate reaction was that the declared abrogation of a defense treaty of twenty-four years standing would have "a tremendously adverse impact upon the entire free world," and that the American government must bear "full responsibility."

Meanwhile, Reagan had fulfilled a commitment he made prior to his Asian trip. He addressed a joint luncheon Committee to Conserve Chinese Culture at a large restaurant in Los Angeles' Chinatown. Most people in the audience had family or business ties with Taiwan. He used the occasion to report on what he had said in his speech in Taipei and to describe his current impressions Taiwan. Regarding the rival government in Peking, he observed, "The U.S. friendship with the people of the Chinese mainland can be developed with care, but this can be done only **if it does not jeopardize our close friendship with the Chinese on Taiwan.** (Emphasis added.)

On January 18,1979, the *New York Times* published an important statement by Reagan, titled "Decency for Taiwan." The issue, he said, was not greater friendship for the people of the China Mainland, but rather policy towards Taiwan and "the methods by which we discharged our responsibilities and keep our word." He then listed a detailed program of necessary guarantees to Taiwan: [1] Continued government---to--- government relations between the United States and Taiwan. [2] Future sale, by law, of defensive arms to Taiwan, thus making government---to---government relations necessary since "weapons sales should not be left to quasi-private arrangements."

On February 10, 1979, Reagan made his customary appearance at the annual dinner of the Conservative Political Action Conference. He addressed himself to the important issues of what troubles the American people and troubles our friends abroad. "Have we become totally unreliable and capricious?" he asked. "Are we so completely disorganized, so lacking in common decency and morality, so motivated by the dictates of the moment that we can, in an instant and by the stroke of a pen, put 17 million people over-the-side and escape the consequences?" He then called for a detailed program of specific guarantees to our friends and allies on Taiwan. Reagan concluded with a warning to the Communist leaders in Peking:

"We wish to live in peace with you, and we shall not interfere in your affairs if you do not intervene in ours. We can help you to modernize and update your economy, and we will do so, consistent with our national security objectives. But, when it comes to those 17 million people on Taiwan, **we emphatically state that so long as they wish to retain their independence** in the world, so long as they declare their unwillingness to be either "liberated" by you or unilaterally "reunited" with you---**then so long will they also have the specific and clear support of the United States of America.** [Emphasis added]

At the 1980 Republican convention in Detroit, Reagan's foreign policy adviser, Richard V. Allen, came armed with a private communication from the government in Taiwan stating that the **1979 Taiwan Relations Act** was acceptable as a basis for its' long range relations with what it hopes would be the new Reagan Administration. Reagan had elicited cheers from campaign supporters with this declaration: "There will be no more Taiwans," There will be no more betrayals of friends by the United States.

When Senator Barry Goldwater another zealous supporter of Taiwan called attention to a dozen violations of the Taiwan Relations Act on the part of the Carter administration and recommended further action by Congress to insure the safety and independence of Taiwan, Governor Reagan approved such action. He knew that the Chinese on Taiwan have violated no treaties, make no deals behind our backs, and uttered no words of disrespect or enmity for the American people. He knew also that they have "liquidated" no landlords, closed no churches, and set up no slave labor camps.

He was keenly aware they have done nothing to deserve the deplorable treatment dealt them by the Carter administration which sailed into office under a brave banner called human rights, but so abruptly "struck its' colors."

It is noteworthy that Ronald Reagan is the only presidential candidate on record in the 1980 election in strong support of the Republic of China. His emotions were deeply engaged in this effort. Any suggestion of abandoning the Chinese on Taiwan, or of subjecting them to insult, deeply offended his sense of loyalty.

"As much as anyone I have known, Reagan attaches himself to a cause rather than people," observed Michael Deaver, a confidant of Reagan for more than twenty years. He seemed assured the Republic of China merits our enduring friendship and highest commendation as a nation that can stand strong and tall on its' own two feet. It is squarely within the American tradition which Ronald Reagan personifies---that this should be so, and anything less is simply not enough for Americans.

During the Presidential campaign, Reagan left little doubt that he was one of those who believed that Jimmy Carter had gone too far in his concessions on Taiwan. On August 25, 1980, in welcoming his running mate, George Bush, back from a visit to China, Reagan said in a formal statement:

> "I felt that a condition of normalization, by itself a sound policy, should have been the retention of a liaison office on Taiwan of equivalent status to the one we had earlier established at Beijing. [Emphasis added]....I would not pretend that the relationship we now have with Taiwan...is not official....It is absurd and not required by the (Taiwan relations) Act that our representatives are not permitted to meet with Taiwanese officials with fairness and dignity."

He also vowed if elected, he would reverse the trend and upgrade U.S.- Taiwan relations by promising that these relations would be placed on an "official" basis. moreover, as President, he would not let "any foreign power" [referring to Communist China] interfere with the execution of the United States as embodied in the Taiwan Relations Act (TRA) passed by overwhelming vote of both Houses of the U.S. Congress. "To do otherwise," he said, "would be a dereliction of my duty as President." This strong statement was issued by the Reagan campaign staff two months before the election. No one could expect, however, that these positions by Reagan would go unchallenged. Critics in the U.S. State Department, as well as Congress, were quick to respond. After all, they flew in the face not only Democratic candidate Carter's actions in China policy, but also of the whole policy toward China as it had been initiated and carried out by Republican Presidents Nixon and Ford with the help of Dr. Henry Kissinger and the entire foreign policy establishment of the U.S. government. They embodied and illustrated well the power of the Nixon-Ford-Kissinger clique in the Party, as well as the dominance within the Eastern wing of the Republican Party, which had worked to defeat the Reagan candidacy in 1976. Such interests as the banking and aviation interests centered in the Eastern part of the United States.

Secretary of State Alexander Haig was not as enthusiastic about Taiwan as President Reagan, but he was the strongest cabinet member who pushed hard for a military buildup of Communist China as a barrier against Soviet expansion. It was vitally important, Haig argued, to the U.S. that the PRC not re-align itself with the Soviet Union; that the U.S. must go to great lengths in making significant concessions to Beijing even at the expense of Taiwan. This act would insure that Beijing cooperate at least tacitly with the U.S. as a strategic counterweight to Russia. Therefore, arms sales to Taiwan should be terminated as they only aggravated the PRC---a key player in the triangular power game. [Emphasis added].

To carry out his desires, Haig instructed several officers in the State Department to prepare secretly a policy document terminating arms sales to Taiwan. When the contents of this document were leaked to some members of Congress, they wasted no time convincing the President it was time to fire Haig.

In his memoirs President Reagan explains how he and Secretary of State Haig differed about Taiwan:

> *"I regarded Taiwan as a loyal, democratic, longtime ally to whom we owed unqualified support. Haig and others at the State Department were so eager to improve relations with the People's Republic of China that they pressed me to back away from this pledge of support. I felt we had an obligation to the people of Taiwan and no one was going to keep up from meeting it."*

Ronald Reagan more than any other former American President admired Taiwan as a friend and loyal ally and proud of its' growing international importance. After leaving the White house, he did something no President had done. He told a Captive Nations Week Conference in Los Angeles that he believed the achievements of the Republic of China on Taiwan will have "profound implications" for the future of all China. **"We in America can never go wrong if we do what is morally right and keep our commitments to Taiwan."** [Emphasis added].

Reagan told the delegates at the opening session on July 15, 1991: "In our relationship with (mainland) China, we should always remember what our Chinese friends on Taiwan have accomplished: "A resource-poor island has become one of the major trading nations in the world, a political transformation no less dramatic than that of Europe has resulted in full-fledge democracy."

Today its' free market economy has propelled the ROC on Taiwan into the 14th largest trading nation in the world. It ranks second in East Asia for trade competitiveness, following only Japan, and has great potential to develop into an Asian-Pacific production center, occording to the Ministry of Economic Affairs. Similar optimism is expressed by the Council for Economic Planning and Development. Citing a report by the World

Bank, the council said Taiwan is expected to emerge as the world's 10th largest economic power by the year 2020, up from its' current ranking of 20th. Taiwan also enjoys a rule of law. It recognizes property rights. It has a viable political opposition and a free press.

When Reagan left the White House a *New York Times / CBS News* poll reported that seven in ten of those polled supported his foreign policy. He was the oldest President in American history, had stayed the course for two terms, the first since Eisenhower to serve the full eight yeat years. Voters had an extraordinary affection for him as a man. They were inspired by his optimism, and they responded to his warmth and humor. Most of all, they respected the fact that he said what he meant, and meant what he said. He told us for the first time that we could win the Cold War---and we did. He got us to stand up to the lie that "history is on the side of tyranny." He's the one who will "live in history," when the pessimists are long forgotten.

"As Reagan's enchantment came to an end," writes former news commentator John Chancellor, "Reagan exited, smiling." And now in January, 1995 Ronald Reagan announced that he has Alzheimer's in a hand-written letter revealing a straightforward honest Reagan touch. I hope he knows how much many Americans admire him for his contribution and defense of the free Chinese people on Taiwan.

As we move closer towards the 21st Century, what can be said about the future prospects of America's role in Asia? In a speech on Sino-American Relations in San Francisco on March 5, 1983, President Reagan's Secretary of State George Shultz gave his audience an encouraging message when he said "...nothing underscores the direct interest of the United States in this region (Asia) more than two simple facts: We trade ;more today with the nations of the Asia Pacific than with any other on earth, and we have three wars in the last forty years. We do not want to fight another and this is a reason why the United States will continue to maintain a presence there."

Also projecting into the future, President Reagan on more than one occasion called the 21St Century the "Pacific Era," a salute to Asia's economic growth. This growth has been stimulated by sound financial management, abundant human resources, and by a strong technological base built on scientific and technical education. Overall, national development has been most pronounced in those countries in which natural economic forces and human potential have been largely unleashed.

The U.S. has important commercial relationships with Taiwan that augments social, cultural and other relations with old friends. Because U.S. policy has proved successful, Washington must remain consistent in implementing the Taiwan Relations Act.

+++++

POSTWAR

AMERICAN POLICY TOWARD CHINA

by Victor T. H. Tsuan, Ph.D.

Since the communist conquest of mainland China, China has been divided into two parts: The Republic of China [hereafter cited as the **ROC**] in Taiwan, and People's Republic of China [thereafter cited as the **PRC**] in the mainland. What has been the American policy toward China during the postwar period?

Chronologically, it can be divided into three stages: 1) The civil war period [1945-49]; 2) The ROC period [1949-78]; 3) The PRC period [1979 to the present].

HISTORICAL BACKGROUND

In analyzing major factors effecting American postwar policy toward China, one must bear in mind the relevance of the historical relationship between the United States and China. The traditional American China policy put emphasis on the freedom of the seas and equality of commercial opportunity among the great powers. In addition, it emphasized educational, diplomatic and philanthropic interests in China by American missionaries. In order to achieve these ends, the United States has always been opposed to the control of China by any foreign power, and in favor of Chinese political independence and territorial integrity. It reached a climax by the turn of the century, when Imperialistic pressures had threatened a division of the Chinese Empire into spheres of influence among other great powers. Secretary of State John Hay invited the powers chiefly concerned with China to accept his "open door" policy which prevented the dissolution of the country, and helped China to regain its sovereignty.

Among the replies from six great powers, Japan went farthest in accepting the principles which Secretary Hay had advanced for preventing European rivals from monopolizing Chinese trade or partitioning China. At that time Japan itself was still too weak to share the benefit beyond Korea, Taiwan, the Pescadores and the Liaotung Peninsula which were under its control as the result of the first Sino-Japanese war [1894-95]. But after the end of the Russo-Japanese war [1904-05], followed by World War I, Japan became the only country which seriously challenged the "open-door" policy. Before the Pearl Harbor incident, on six occasions this policy was restated by the State Department.

The main antagonism in the ultimate conflict between the United States and Japan was over the fate of China: Japan bent on conquering China, the United States on preserving China's territorial integrity and political independence. After several months of fruitless negotiations, war finally came to Pearl Harbor.

The importance of China in Asia, especially after the defeat of Japan, has been recognized. President Franklin D. Roosevelt and Secretary of State Cordell Hull anticipated that China would fill the power vacuum which was created by the Japanese defeat. A strong and peace-loving China would safeguard American interests and national security in the Western Pacific. This objective required urgent diplomatic maneuvers to unite the rival Chinese groups and to create a strong, united and democratic China. Both Winston S. Churchill and Joseph V. Stalin were skeptical about a satisfactory solution.

Following the end of World War II, for a period of approximately five years the united States was the most powerful nation of the world. With its unique economic position, military supremacy, and its sole possession of nuclear weapons, it would be reasonable to assume that its immediate postwar foreign policy toward any single nation in Asia would have had no difficulty. If it had been based on the same principles of dealing with the communist threat in Asia as well as in Europe, it would have been successful. Before this unique opportunity came to an end, however, American policy toward China had run into a stalemate.

Finally, the successful atomic explosion by the Soviet union in June, 1949, and the emergence of communist China in Asia among other communist countries opposing the united States, caused the complete collapse of President Roosevelt's wartime policy of establishing China as the foremost power in the Far East. Therefore, American policy toward China after World War II has been a complete failure.

THE CIVIL WAR PERIOD [1945-49]

At the end of World War II, the United States government, not fully comprehending the true nature of the internal crisis in China, found itself in a dilemma. At first it urged the Nationalist government to conclude the Sino-Soviet Treaty of Friendship and Alliance of August 14, 1945, confirming the secret wartime agreement made at Yalta. By so doing, the State Department considered that the Soviet union had accepted definite limitations on its activities in China, and was committed to withhold all its aid from the Chinese communists. This proved to be optimistic thinking. In fact, the Chinese concession to the Soviet Union in Outer Mongolia and Manchuria facilitated the Chinese communists, with the help of the Soviet Union, in the conquest of the Chinese mainland in 1949. This conquest was a major blow to American policy toward China.

On November 27, 1945, President Harry S. Truman announced that he had appointed General George C. Marshall as his special envoy to China. Marshall was instructed to bring about understanding and cooperation between the rival Chinese nationalists and communists, and to reconstruct a coalition government for China. Unfortunately, his mission was utterly unrealistic and doomed to failure. As a matter of fact, the United States was unintentionally aiding the Chinese communists in the critical years of 1946-47 while trying to pose as mediator. General Marshall was disappointed and felt frustrated in his mission to China. Upon his return to Washington he was appointed Secretary of State by President Truman. Marshall took an oath to become secretary of State on January 21, 1947. Since then there was a sudden shift of United States policy toward China, namely, from active intervention in internal Chinese affairs to partial disinvolvement. Marshall's recall from China was followed by the withdrawal of American personnel from the Executive headquarters, and several thousand American troops, and the cutting off of economic and military aid to the nationalist government.

Between the end of Marshall's mission on January 6, 1947, and the outbreak of the Korean war on June 25, 1950, the United States government postponed basic decisions to avoid any involvement in the Chinese civil conflict. The Truman administration was afraid of the general communist threat to its security and the possibility of a Third World War only in Western Europe. Its anti-Communist containment policy beginning with the announcement of the Truman doctrine on March 12, 1947, as well as the Marshall plan for American aid, and the establishment of the North Atlantic Treaty Organization to defend against possible communist aggression, applied only to Western Europe and its adjacent areas. The United States did not extend its general program and strategy to Asia before the Korean war broke out

The lightning that struck in the Far East rather than in Western Europe may hardly have been anticipated by the Truman administration. Therefore, since postwar American foreign policy strove for the realization of two utterly different objectives in Europe and Asia, one of them was bound to fail.

THE REPUBLIC OF CHINA PERIOD [1949-1978]

After the establishment of the PRC on October 1, 1949, Secretary of State Dean G. Acheson, while anticipating the loss of Taiwan to the Chinese communists, endeavored to sell the public on the idea that the island had no strategic value for American defense in the Western Pacific. Consequently his effort was to disentangle the United States from the collapsed Nationalist Government. This policy offered the Republican opposition to Truman and Acheson a rare opportunity: they blamed the administration for the debacle.

On the other hand, Acheson tried to stir up dissension between Communist China and the Soviet union. He wished to keep Red China away from full participation in the Soviet bloc, and was awaiting a clash between the Soviet Union and Communist China. On January 12, 1950, in an important address before the national Press Club in Washington, he said:

"What is happening in China is that the Soviet union is detaching the northern provinces of China from China and is attaching them to the Soviet Union."

Meanwhile he [Acheson] decided to contain communism in Asia outside mainland China, especially in Japan and Southeast Asia. Such a policy presented obvious difficulties. Since the range of Chinese communist influence has been far beyond the confines of China's border, it necessitated a direct confrontation with the interests of the major foreign powers in Asia. By not making concessions where feasible, and holding fast where necessary, in addition to the Chinese communist assault on "capitalist imperialism," Acheson was unable to prevent Communist China from becoming a Soviet ally in February, 1950.

1950 was a crucial year in American policy toward China. Two major decisions were made by the Truman administration. On January 5, 1950, President Truman announced his decision that no more military aid or advice would be provided for the defense of Taiwan. Secretary Acheson specified certain areas in Asia from the Aleutians through Japan and Ryukyus to the Philippines are vital to the security of the united States and by so doing he implied that this country would fight to defend them. Neither Taiwan nor South Korea was included.

It was widely interpreted that the administration did not regard the defense of these areas against a possible communist attack as vital. Of course, no one can be sure whether a stronger warning would have prevented the North Korean aggression, yet it is clear, in retrospect, that the danger of military invasions in South Korea and Taiwan had seen under-estimated by the Truman administration. Critics in the Congress charged that Secretary Acheson had given a "green light" to the communists, especially in South Korea.

But, following the outbreak of the Korean war, the United States faced a situation where the stakes were extremely high, and rapid decisions involving major national commitments and risks were called for. President Truman immediately ordered American forces into the Korean fighting and announced his new decision on China on June 27, 1950 as follows:

> *"The occupation of Formosa by communist forces would be a direct threat to the security of the Pacific area and to the United States forces performing their lawful and necessary functions in that area. Accordingly, I have ordered the Seventh fleet to prevent any attack on Formosa."*

In response to Truman's sudden decision, President Chiang Kai-shek of the ROC proposed to President Truman to send 33,000 Chinese nationalist troops to Korea. This proposal was cautiously rejected by the United States.

In a stroke Truman changed the controversial "hands-off Taiwan" policy. Thus American commitment to the ROC in Taiwan had been reinforced as a result of the Korean war. It was the foundation of American policy toward China before President Jimmy Carter's announcement of normalization of relations between the United States and the PRC on December 15, 1978. It had stabilized the status quo between the ROC and the PRC on the one hand, and became a stumbling block in maintaining international peace in East Asia on the other.

The Truman administration's containment policy toward China lasted more than a decade. Since 1955, during the Eisenhower Administration, periodic exchange of conversations between Chinese communist and American government representatives had taken place at Geneva and Warsaw without any concrete results. Influenced perhaps by the "Bay of Pigs" fiasco, President John F. Kennedy took a more cautious approach in dealing with Communist China. During the Johnson administration, China policy was modified to "containment without isolation." The shift, however, was accompanied by no tangible initiatives and induced no reciprocity from Communist China.

The major change of the postwar American policy toward China under the Nixon administration was based on two assumptions: 1) Communist China's cooperation was considered as a precondition for ending the war in Vietnam. 2) The widening conflict between Communist China and the Soviet union had increased the possibility of improving relations between the united States and Communist China. Therefore, the National Security Council under the Nixon administration discussed the new China policy in August, 1969. The decision was made that an improvement of relations with Beijing was possible without abandoning Taiwan, and without jeopardizing relations with Moscow. Initial steps were taken to relax certain restrictions on trade and travel, and the Warsaw ambassadorial talks were revived.

After the announcement that President Richard M. Nixon would visit Beijing the following year, Communist China was admitted to the United Nations on October 25, 1971. The permanent Security Council seat was offered as well. In accordance with the Joint Shanghai Communique' of February 27, 1972, exchange of liaison officers between Washington and Beijing took place in May, 1973. In addition, there has been an exchange of scientific, medical and cultural groups. On the other hand, the ROC was ousted from the United Nations, followed by the withdrawal of recognition by several non-communist countries. It was a severe blow to a faithful American ally.

Meanwhile Sino-American hostility continued. Communist leaders made contemptuous statements about the "capitalist world." In addition, the Watergate scandal forced Nixon to resign in August, 1974; he was succeeded by President Gerald R. Ford who visited Beijing at the end of 1975. Due to the leadership crisis in Communist China after the deaths of Zhou Enlai and Mao Zedong in 1976, normalization of relations between the United States and Communist China was further delayed.

Having learned a bitter lesson from their defeat on the mainland, and realizing that Taiwan is poorly endowed in resources, nationalist Chinese leaders have paid special attention to drastic changes of political, economic and social conditions in Taiwan. They hoped for a counterattack and recovery of the mainland. The overwhelming majority of the citizenry was ready for change. With American economic and military assistance since 1950, in two decades Taiwan was transformed from an agricultural to an industrial society; and in one generation, the original backward island was transformed into one of Asia's most prosperous and advanced areas. The government of the ROC, under Presidents Chiang Kai-shek and Chiang Ching-Kuo's leadership, has established a splendid record, and its amazing economic development has been recognized and widely acclaimed as a "miracle."

The Sino-Soviet split developed in the late 1950's, and continued steadily. This split finally led to military confrontation. Meanwhile Communist China was determined to become an independent nuclear power. It achieved its first nuclear explosion in October, 1964, followed by a second in May, 1965. Its first guided missile occurred in October, 1966, and its first hydrogen bomb was exploded in June, 1967. Thus, the increasing caution of the superpowers made their respective allies apprehensive. Sino-Soviet border incidents began to occur in 1969, and Soviet forces in Asia were built up accordingly. By the end of that year, Communist China's relations with the Soviet union worsened. Postwar American policy toward the ROC may have outlived its usefulness. As a result, the Nixon-Kissinger policy of seeking normal relations with the PRC began. replacement of Taipei by Beijing and the effort to preserve the integrity of Taiwan as an independent entity became the ultimate goal of American policy toward China.

THE PEOPLE'S REPUBLIC OF CHINA PERIOD [1979 to the present]

The establishment of diplomatic relations between the United States and PRC on January 1, 1979 under the Carter administration gave a mighty boost to Communist China's feeling of security. Consequently, it notified the Soviet Union in April, 1979 that the Sino-Soviet Treaty of Friendship, Alliance and Mutual Assistance would be abrogated upon expiration on February 14, 1980.

Until today [1996], the United States and the PRC's relations have improved to some extent, with mutual trade expanded, exchange of experts and students increased, and plant, equipment, as well as technological assistance being applied for in a wide variety of projects. however, differences in social system, ideology and world outlook have led the leaders of both governments to distrust the motives of the other in their dealings. The fact remains that a genuine understanding, no matter how desirable, will be most difficult to achieve. Moreover, the prospect of a leadership change in Beijing might have a reverse effect. It seems that the United States is sacrificing long range concerns for short term solution. Hence in appraising the American policy toward China in the post-war period, one must conclude that a faithful ally in east Asia remains a useful counter force to any future communist expansion. It is also in the American national interest to strengthen the economic and military power of the ROC in Taiwan as a practical balancing force. The enactment of the Taiwan relations Act of April 10, 1979 does serve such a purpose.

In the near future, if Beijing's foreign policy does not change, and no concrete results emerge in the rapprochement attempt between the United States and the PRC, or no drastic change in the leadership of PRC, we can reasonably expect the status quo for some time. With the collapse of communism in Eastern Europe and the former Soviet union, the cold war in Europe may now have been won. The global cold war, however, is by no means over and the future is uncertain. The PRC and Japan continue to pose a major threat to American interests in Asia. If we accept the idea that American hegemony in Asia as a Pacific power is not viable at present, what kind of role does the American public expect its government to play in Asia after the demise of the Soviet Union? Americans have come to believe, slowly, reluctantly, and only after bitter experiences in Korea and Vietnam, that the communist threat in the Far East and Southeast Asia is real, and further communist expansion must be checked. The postwar error of American policy toward China has chiefly stemmed from a failure to understand the scope and the complexity of the Chinese problems.

Chinese communists rose to power by tyrannizing the people with their inhuman rule. Under its system of one-party socialism, it exhausted possibilities for promoting freedom and democracy, even though it had briefly tolerated them before the Tiananmen incident in June 1989. On the other hand, Zhou Enlai's proposal for the Four Modernizations in 1964, in the areas of industry, agriculture, science-and-technology, and defense have been carried out since 1979 by then Vice Premier Deng Xiaoping, but in practice they have proven to be limited to a small region, unreal, shallow and transitory.

At present, the situation in the PRC is greatly unstable, and popular discontent over the totalitarian government is fueled further by the Chinese people's growing awareness of recent developments in Eastern Europe and the former Soviet Union. The dissolution of communism abroad cannot help but further de-legitimize a political system that seems increasingly to be disintegrating from the top down. sooner or later Chinese people will force the communists to give up their hold on power. realizing the imminent danger, the Chinese communist government lately has increased its military budget more than ten percent annually since 1989. Since Deng Xiaoping has made the reunification of China one of the major goals of his leadership, it seems possible that if the ROC continues to refuse accepting his **"one country, two systems"** proposal, he might exert military pressure against Taiwan, such as a naval blockade.

The Bush Administration's European policy had seen successes from the collapse of communism in Eastern Europe and the former Soviet Union to the Gulf War. On the other hand, its realistic and workable policy toward China was much to be desired. The Clinton Administration's foreign policy in general has been somewhat ad interim and driven by domestic politics. It's policy toward China has not eliminated the differences in perspective between the ROC and PRC, and in certain measures have even added new tensions and problems.

In actuality, and the policies based upon it, inasmuch as PRC's economic miracle in recent years, American companies have invested more than S7 billion there since 1979, and export about $9 billion worth of goods to PRC annually. The United States also imports nearly $40 billion worth of Chinese goods, making PRC America's sixth largest trading partner. Therefore, the Clinton Administration will certainly remain committed to renewing PRC's most-favored-nations trading status this spring. [1996] On the other hand, Sino-American relations have been deteriorating since the United States recognized Vietnam and allowed ROC's President Lee Teng-Hui to visit the United States last summer. [1995]

Lately PRC has up to 200,000 troops of the People's Liberation Army in Fujian Province, planning a month long exercise along the coast across from Taiwan. The dangers posed to regional peace might be avoided with Washington's firm stand in handling such threat. In the final analysis, Sino-American relations cannot improve drastically in the long run, unless China becomes united and free from communism.

+++++

Sun Tzu said in "The Art of War" over 2300 years ago:

"National unity is an essential requirement of victorious war. This could be attained only under a government which was devoted to the people's welfare and did not oppress them."

An associate of Sun Tzu--- Wu Ch'i's "Art of War " 430-381 B.C. in Section V by Wu Tzu writes:

"There are five matters which give rise to military operations:

First;   The struggle for fame.
Second;   The struggle for advantage.
Third;   The accumulation of animosity.
Fourth,   Internal disorder, and
Fifth;   Famine."

Chapter IV

CHINESE IMMIGRANTS IN THE

UNITED STATES

Archival Records of Chinese Immigrants

by Betty Lee Sung, Ph.D.

ONE OF THE MOST COMPELLING TASKS of the Asian Americanist is the retrieval of our rightful history in this country. Until recent times, it has been omitted, distorted, glossed over, made mysterious, or fictionalized. There are huge gaps and missing links, which came about due to harsh immigration laws. It seemed as if the period between the end of the nineteenth century and the beginning of the twentieth was one of these gaps for the Chinese in the United States.

Their earlier history during the Gold Rush years is fairly well documented, and so is the period when the Chinese formed the main labor force in the building of the transcontinental railroad. However, after the Chinese Exclusion Act of 1882 went into effect, those Chinese already in the United States found themselves unwanted and hounded. They tried to be as unobtrusive as possible to the point of becoming invisible. To have drawn attention to themselves would have invited inquiry, harassment, persecution, and perhaps deportation. At the same time, with a substantial decrease in their numbers, public interest in them faded.

Those who remained in this country kept to themselves, but the lure of the "Mountain of Gold" --- the United States as a land of riches --- continued its draw. New immigrants wanted in, and ingenious ways were devised to circumvent the Exclusion Act. Naturally these extra-legal immigrants did not want to draw attention to themselves either, so secrecy shrouded the Chinese communities in this country. Survival at the time necessitated this blackout of information, so little in the way of recorded information comes down to us.

Unlike the Polish immigrants that Florian Znaniecki wrote about or even the Japanese immigrants documented by Yuji Ichioka, the early Chinese in the United States were generally illiterate or barely literate. They seldom wrote letters home, and when they did they sought the services of professional letter writers. These letters were highly stylized, in uniform format, and contained little personal information. They said little except "I am sending you money. I am well and I hope you are too." So recorded information from this source as well is almost non existent. Even if some letters or correspondence were kept by the families in China and survived into the mid-twentieth century, they were probably destroyed during the communist revolution when any connection with someone in the United States was suspect and even dangerous.

With this huge gap, the prospect of recreating the history of the Chinese in the United States was gloomy and discouraging. There were few records and few documents, and the people who lived during those times were long gone. Then lately in my research, I came across an item revealing that the U.S. Archives contained a repository of Chinese immigration records going back to the min-1800s for the New York region. I tracked the records to an archival repository in Bayonne, N.J. where I found 581 boxes crammed full of files of every Chinese who entered the country through the New York region ports of entry. These records spanned a period of almost a hundred years. The discovery was like stumbling across an archeological find of antiquity.

These files belong to the U.S. Archives and should have been retrievable in some manner. When I asked to see the boxes containing the earliest files, however, I was confronted with a blank stare. No one knew what order the files were in except under names, and the romanization of Chinese names were questionable at best. The files were not chronological. Box No.1 did not contain the files of the earliest immigrants and Box 581 the latest. Simply stated, there was no discernible order to the data. I saw a wall of boxes from floor to ceiling containing a good portion of our lost history but no way to get at the information except to wade through the entire lot.

Because of my investigation and interest, Dr. Robert Morris, director of the New York Regional Archives, began to rummage through the files. As an historian, he was fascinated by the materials he found. Together, he and I began to think of ways to access this data.

In 1990, I wrote a proposal to the Chiang Ching Kuo Foundation, suggesting that the files be put on a database format for ready retrieval under date of entry, name, subject heading and other key words. Without some system of retrieval, these files were too cumbersome to utilize in any fashion. The Chiang Ching Kuo Foundation readily saw the value of this storehouse of information regarding the Chinese in the United States and immediately awarded me a grant of $50,000 to initiate the project in 1993. I was awarded another grant from the National Endowment for the Humanities.

The records are voluminous. Each box contains about 25 ;to 50 files. Information from each file must be read and entered into the computer. The work requires rapid reading knowledge of Chinese and English, conversion of Chinese dates into Western dates, some knowledge of Chinese American history, coding of the Chinese names using the four-corner system, and computer literacy --- a tall order indeed. We are utilizing a dBase 4 program so that researchers, historians, and any potential user can call up the information wanted speedily and efficiently, thus encouraging scholars to tap into this historical treasure trove. When the database discs are complete, copies will be made available to other regional archives and libraries, thus enabling scholars throughout the country to utilize the database.

The files contain original documents like exit permits from the Chinese Emperor, certificates of identity that the Chinese were required to carry, reentry permits from the U.S. government, photos, and extensive interrogation records that provide valuable personal information and social history of that time. Already, a cursory examination of some of the files has brought to light a number of events that may challenge existing Chinese American history. For example, it is commonly believed that the earliest Chinese settlers in New York City came after the completion of the transcontinental railroad and that they came from the Western states. Dome of the records reveal that Chinese immigrants may have entered New York directly before completion of the railroad, and they came by ship from the Caribbean or overland from Canada. There extensive family histories that can be pieced together from the interrogations.

The exciting aspect of these records is that they can be used for genealogical research. The early Chinese were not a vocal or verbal people. family members did not know about what their fathers and granfathers did in this country. If these menfolk made trips to China, their experiences would be chronicled in the interrogation that each one had to go through to regain entry into the United States. Almost all the files have photos, so descendants can see what their fore-bears look like.

The files go back to the latter part of the 19th century and extend into the min-20th century through the cofession period of the 1950s. They cover approximately a hundred years of Chinese American historty. These files cover the New York retion only. Howevfer, there are similar files in the twelve archival regions in the United States. After I discovered the New York files, other retions began tracking down their Chinese immigrant records. Now scholars and researchers from other parts of the country havbe found similiar caches of Chinese immigrant records in other major ports of entry like San Franscisco, Seattle, Philadelphia and Boston. They have inquired about our project and hope to do something similar with files. Already Seattle was awarded a Chiang Ching Kuo Foundation grant to commence work on their files and San Francisco may be following suit.

When the project is completed, scholars and researchers can readily tap into this rich treasure-trove of original documents to recreate our history.

+++++

CHINESE IMMIGRANTS CREATE THEIR OWN JOBS

by Betty Lee Sung, Ph.D.

Periodically, the American people become paranoiac and start blaming immigrants and attacking immigration as the source of the country's ill, as witness Proposition 187 in California and pending bills in Congress, which would drastically curtail the numbers admitted and deprive even legal immigrants basic services traditionally accorded newcomers. Will immigrants "sink the boat," as Peter Brimelow charges in his book, *Alien Nation*? With a Mellon foundation grant the Regional Plan Association undertook a study to find out, looking at the major immigrants coming to the Tri-State region, and I undertook the research on the Chinese.

The metropolitan area of the New York-New Jersey-Connecticut Tri-State region is a favorite destination of Chinese immigrants. More come to this region than all Chinese immigrants to Los Angeles and San Francisco combined. From 1980 to 1990, Chinese population in this region doubled from 164,000 to 329,000. Almost half of this came from immigration. About 70 percent are found in the urban core of Manhattan, Queens, and Brooklyn, although dispersion to the outlying counties is taking place. [See Table 1]

Table 1

Chinese Population in the New York Tri-State Region, 1980-1990 and Chinese Immigration, 1983-1991

Place	Population		Pct	Immigration
	1980	1990	Increase	1983 1991
NYC Total	124,372	240,014	93	85,881
Bronx	4,884	6,693	37	2,283
Brooklyn	26,067	68,905	164	20,960
Manhattan	52,165	72,277	39	33,414
Queens	39,526	87,001	120	28,038
Staten Island	1,730	5,138	197	1,186
Long Island 2 Cty	8,500	17,924	111	4,926
Mid Hudson 7 Cty	6,507	12,684	95	3,015
New Jersey 14 Ct	20,907	52,334	150	14,116
Conn. 3 Cty	3,293	6,513	98	1,603
31 Counties	**163,579**	**329,469**	**101**	**109,541**

Source: U.S. Census and Immigration and Naturalization Service

Factors propelling this influx are the Immigration Act of 1965, the lifting of the "Bamboo Curtain," the pending return of Hong Kong to Mainland China, the fear of a Communist invasion of Taiwan, the political repression in China, and the quest for higher education in the United states. The push factors have been as strong as the pull factors.

Immigrants More Diverse

Today's Chinese immigrants are extremely diverse, quite different from the old-timers who were primarily men from the Canton Delta area. Now they from all provinces in China as well as Hong Kong and Taiwan. In fact, many immigrants from Malaysia, Singapore, Thailand, Burma, Indonesia and Philippines as well as refugees from Vietnam, Laos and Cambodia are ethnic Chinese. However, for purposes of this study, the numbers refer only to Chinese from Mainland China, Hong Kong and Taiwan.

More women than men come, so that the sex ratio is now in balance, whereas it used to be terribly lopsided favoring the men. Two-fifths of Chinese immigrants are under the age of 25, making them a young and vigorous group.[Dept. of City Planning: 1992] They are or become a highly educated group. According to the 1990 census, 32 percent of all foreign born Chinese 16 years and over in the Tri-State Region have a college degree or better. At the other end of the scale, 38 percent have less than a high school education, which creates a bimodal curve on the socioeconomic scale giving the Chinese a dual image. **[See Table 2]**

The bimodal profile is a reflection of U.S. immigration policy, that of family reunification, skills preference, and refugees. Most of those coming in under family reunification are from Mainland China where they have been educationally deprived un Communist rule. However, a large contingent of China's intellectual elite were here in the United States in 1989 when the Tiananmen incident occurred. President Bush's executive order permitted them to stay. In fear of Communist take-over, immigrants from Hong Kong and Taiwan brought with them capital and know-how to start their own businesses or enter the professions.

Illegals?

The *Golden Venture* incident in which 287 Chinese tried to smuggle ashore in Long Island in 1993 brought exaggerated charges that hordes of Chinese were entering the country illegally. A *New York Times* editorial (June 9, 1993) read: "The *Golden Venture* Plus 100,000" How did 287 inflate to 100,000? A factual study done by the New York City Planning Commission revealed that the Chinese are low in the scale of illegals. For a country with more than a billion in population, Chinese illegals are fewer than those for tiny nation like Israel. [Sontag: 1993]

The labor force participation rate for Chinese in the Tri-State Region is 72 percent for those 16 years and over. **[See Table 2]** A higher rate would result if the numbers were for those 25 years and over because in their late teens and early twenties Chinese youths are still enrolled in high school or college. Using the later age cut-off, the male labor force participation rate is **88** percent for males and **71** percent for females. [PUMS File: 1990] This high rate for females, even those in the child-rearing ages, reveals that two earners are needed to maintain an immigrant family.

Chinese Create Jobs

A common charge leveled at immigrants is that they take away jobs from native Americans. On the contrary, the Chinese have created their own jobs as well as peripheral jobs for others. Essentially the Chinese are concentrated in four general areas of employment: the garment industry, the restaurant industry, the ethnic niche, and mainstream occupations.

Apparel manufacturing is a $10 billion industry in New York employing about 100,000 workers. [Garment Industry Development Corps: 1992] About 40,000 of these are Chinese, mostly women garment factory workers. This was an industry almost lost to New York City for lack of labor and cheaper imports. The influx of Chinese females since the late 1960s has supplied the industry with a continuous stream of workers. Almost as quickly, the Chinese moved into contracting, setting up their own garment factories. There are approximately 600 to 700 such factories producing about a third of all garments manufactured in New York. Most are small enterprises. The combined payroll in the unionized factories runs to about $450 million annually [John Wang Interview] substantially sustaining the Chinese immigrant population. The retention of the apparel industry in New York also generates peripheral jobs in the fashion industry.

Chinese restaurants are a ubiquitous sight in New York City and elsewhere. They are the second most important economic activity for the Chinese. These restaurants feature China's culinary art. The American public is treated to new foods and exotic flavors, adding a new dimension to their eating experience. There are more than 2,000 restaurants scattered throughout the Tri-State Region. The seafood, meat, vegetables, linen and other suppliers of the restaurants enlarge upon the jobs created by these restaurants. Without Chinese immigrants, this industry would not exist. About half of Chinese residents in New York work either the garment industry or restaurant industry operated either as family enterprises or small businesses. [Ong and Umemoto: 1994]

The rapid increase in Chinese population in the region laid a market base broad enough to enable co-ethnics to serve one another. These are stores selling all kinds of merchandise and foodstuff to services such as doctors, accountants, travel agents, insurance brokers and the like. The ethnic niche in employment calls for concentration of businesses and services. That helps account for the expansive growth of Chinatowns in Lower Manhattan, in flushing, Queens and Sunset Park in Brooklyn. Buying from co-ethnics and servicing one another provide substantial employment for Chinese immigrants who do not have the language facility or knowledge of mainstream options.

Community Revitalization

With the influx of immigrants, New York's original Chinatown in lower Manhattan quickly became saturated and spun off satellites. In the establishment of these satellite Chinatowns, the Chinese have usually moved into transitional areas in decline and reinvigorated the neighborhoods and local business. Both Flushing in Queens and Sunset Park in Brooklyn are prime examples of community revitalization. Wendy Weber, Associate Director of the Downtown Flushing Development Corporation said, "Flushing during the 1970s was a depressed area. It was the Asian investment that turned the area around." [Gottlieb; 1985] Regarding Sunset Park, one elderly lady said, "I feel safer in the neighborhood now that the Chinese have moved in."

Ethnic Enclave Economy

All three fields of economic described above can be grouped under the heading "ethnic enclave economy," a concept developed extensively by Alejandro Portes and Min Zhou. Zhou argues in her book, *Chinatown* (1992) that this economic behavior is ethnically based. Owners and workers are Chinese, often close or extended family members. Capital comes from pooled resources. Working conditions and organizational set-up may follow Chinese customs. The employer-employee relationship may be very paternalistic. Goods and service may be provided to an ethnic clientele, but there is an export sector where output is destined for the larger market, as in the garment and restaurant industries. The ethnic enclave economy has absorbed Chinese immigrants to the extent that the unemployment rate is low---a mere 5.1 percent in 1990 when the City rate was close to 11 percent. The public assistance rate is an inconsequential 3.3 percent. This explodes another popular myth that immigrants are heavily into public dole. [See Table 2]

The well-educated and professionally trained can move into mainstream occupations. As noted above, about one-third of Chinese immigrants are college graduates or better. However, English-speaking ability limits their options. For the Tri-State region, about three out of four foreign born Chinese say they are limited English speaking. [See Table 2]. That is why so many Chinese are found in the math, science and technology fields where English is less of a problem. Almost a quarter of all science and engineering degrees awarded in 1990 were conferred upon Asian Americans. There are presently over a quarter million Asian American scientists and engineers, and Chinese Americans comprise a goodly proportion of these. [Ong and Blumenburg: 1994]. In this technology age, America needs these skills and expertise. Yet native born Americans tend to shy away from these fields, while Asian Americans have filled a vital gap in keeping this country in the forefront in technology.

Chinese Americans seem to be moving into a new fields -- that of international trade. For nearly a quarter of a century, China was under a self-imposed isolation, and her borders were closed. Those restrictions are now gone. The Chinese economy is exploding at double digit rates, and demand for American goods is growing. For example, the Boeing Company thinks that China alone will need 800 new planes costing about $40 billion dollars. Microsoft estimates that exports to Asia are expanding at the rate of 60 percent a year. [Newsweek: 1993] International trade need not be on a grand scale. Small entrepreneurs with knowledge of Chinese and English and familiarity with both countries are stepping into middlemen positions and doing a brisk trade on their own.

Reverse Migration

With the economy booming in the Far East, reverse migration is taking place, particularly to Taiwan and Hong Kong as well. Computer scientists, engineers, technology experts are returning to their homeland where they find good jobs and salaries awaiting them Those who may have contemplated emigrating to the United States are finding opportunities right at home. Along with the lessening of political oppression, there is no need to go abroad.

Conclusion

In conclusion, the influx of Chinese immigrants has been very beneficial to the Tri-State Region. They have not taken away jobs, rather they have salvaged the No. one manufacturing industry for New York City and they have created a whole new cuisine for the American palate, making jobs for themselves and for peripheral industries as well. They have filled an important gap in the scientific and high tech fields. They are not a drain on public coffers. Both their unemployment rate and public assistance rate are extremely low.

Policy Recommendations

In this day and age, the world runs on information. Without reliable information to base decisions, the outcome can only be haphazard and chancy. For example, little is known about this large group of Chinese newcomers to the Tri-State Region. Local government statistics lump the Chinese under the general category of Asians or others. Some agencies ignore the fact that Asians are among us or they have not caught up. Census data must often be reworked from tapes when specific information in a definite locality is needed. Such was the case for the numbers in this presentation. A Mellon grant to the Regional Plan Association gave us these statistics, otherwise they would not have been available in published form. My first recommendation is for government agencies or other data collectors to include Asians or Chinese as a statistical category and make it possible for researchers to diaggregate the numbers if any one group is under study.

Scholars should be encouraged to do more studies on the Chinese to provide the information needed. New York is rich in institutions of higher learning, and none is more suited than the City University of New York, where a research institute of Asian American Studies could and should be established to serve as a data collecting organization and a "think tank." One of the first subjects for this Institute to undertake would be to come up with an economic ic development plan for the Chinese community as well as the other Asian groups. As pointed out in this presentation, half of the Chinese labor force is engaged in either the garment or restaurant industries. The Chinese must diversify. The garment industry continues to decline and Chinese restaurants are saturated. Plans must be made for the future. Left to their own devices without proper data to guide them, the Chinese suffer the consequences of trial and error and are highly vulnerable. A research institute can address and ameliorate the problems confronting a group undergoing adaptation to a new homeland.

One of the most pressing needs of Chinese immigrants is their limited English-speaking ability. The few programs teaching English in Chinatowns are overscribed. If better access to lessons either in more classes or through the media could be provided, that would be an investment that would be repaid many times over.

An American attitude, which needs to be re-examined, is that high tech, advanced science, well-paying jobs are for U.S. workers, while the lowly manufacturing jobs can be relegated to under-developed nations. This kind of thinking has created a vacuum of jobs in the sectors in this country where the alternatives for the less educated and skilled are to be unemployed or go on public dole, creating an underclass of malcontents looking for scapegoats and targeting immigrants. The United States needs jobs at all levels, not just the top.

A very short-sighted policy would be to drastically curtail immigration. This is a nation of immigrants who have brought new blood and vigor to the United States. As seen in this presentation, immigrants like the Chinese have been beneficial to the Tri-State Region economy, in no way detracting from it.

+++++

Table 2

**Economic Characteristics of the Foreign Born Chinese 16 Years and Over
in the Tri-State Region by Percent, 1990**

	New York City (5 Boros)	Long Island (2 Counties)	Mid Hudson (7 Counties)	New Jersey (14 Counties)	Connecticut (3 Counties)	Total (32 Counties)
Total F.B. Population = 100 Pct.	136,029	9,124	7,099	31,105	3,729	187,086
Labor Force Part	70.0%	71.4%	70.5%	74.3%	80.7%	71.6%
Unemploym't Rate	5.7%	2.9%	3.5%	3.5%	2.9%	5.1%
Self Emloyed	9.4%	17.5%	17.1%	11.0%	6.7%	10.3%
Limited Engl Spking	78.1%	64.4%	56.4%	57.3%	46.3%	72.5%
Public Assist Rate	3.8%	0.9%	1.6%	2.2%	0.8%	3.3%
Occupation						
Mgr/Professional	25.4%	51.2%	63.1%	59.3%	54.9%	34.5%
Sales/Clerical	23.6%	24.9%	14.3%	23.3%	14.7%	23.1%
Service	19.4%	12.7%	16.4%	8.1%	20.4%	17.0%
Blue Collar	31.6%	14.2%	6.2%	9.2%	10.0%	25.5%
Education						
Hi School or Less	45.9%	16.6%	17.0%	13.3%	19.3%	37.5%
Hi School Grad	18.0%	18.8%	10.9%	12.0%	10.2%	16.6%
Some College	13.2%	16.5%	16.2%	13.7%	12.6%	13.5%
College Grad +	22.9%	48.0%	55.9%	61.0%	57.9%	32.4%

Source: 1990 Census PUMS File   Note: In the Census, foreign-born Chinese incluses those born in China, Hong Kong and Taiwan

91

Chapter V

QUEST FOR FREEDOM &

DEMOCRACY

FORTIETH ANNIVERSARY

Of The

KOREAN WAR ARMISTICE

SPEECH
by

John Kirk Singlaub,
Major General, U.S. Army [Ret]

Today [1993] marks a significant event in the history of this nation, but more importantly in the history of the Republic of Korea. It is important, as I will attempt to show.........to the entire world.

Forty years ago today [1953] a formal Armistice was signed at Panmunjom; the major fighting stopped, the troops withdrew two kilometers each, but the conflict continued and is still in effect today. No peace treaty was ever signed.

Two years earlier, on 10 July 1951, a truce was declared, and the Communists started their deceptive policy of "negotiating while fighting". This is Communist policy. This is why many of our casualties occur during cease-fires.

The success of a major U.N. counteroffensive earlier that year had convinced them that they should start this so-called negotiating effect. This has proven to be a typical Communist response to tactical defeats.

During these negotiations, the single most important issue which held up the completion of the Armistice Agreement was the principle of voluntary repatriation. No prisoner would be forced to return to his country of origin against his will. The U.S. army after W.W.II was ordered by Washington to forcibly turn over to the Soviets tens of thousands of refugees from the U.S.S.R. Most were killed or sent off to the gulags. This was known as "Operation Keelhaul".

The final release of the POW's took place on 23 Jan 1954, following 90 days of Red enticement and intimidation. On that day, 14,000 Chinese and 8,000 Koreans chose freedom over a return to their homes in the PRC or North Korea. The U.S. held 101,000 North Koreans and 20,000 Chinese POW's. Of these 33,000 North Korean and 14,000

Chinese refused to return to their homelands. The Korean prisoners were released as civilians in South Korea. The Chinese prisoners were taken to Taiwan where they integrated easily into the population. This date, 23 January, is celebrated in Taiwan and Korea as **World Freedom Day.**

The Communists were surprised that the U.S. responded to the invasion with ground troops along with air and naval forces.

The courageous act by President Harry Truman taught the Communists, be they Soviet, Chinese or Korean, that the United States would not accept the overt invasion of a U.S. ally.

The Soviets understood from that response that they could not expand their empire by overt aggression, whether directly with the Soviet Armed Forces of indirectly through the use of surrogates.

The Korean War has been called the "Forgotten War". While that label may pertain to the general public and its understanding or remembrance of the war, there are many aspects of the war which will never be forgotten by the participants on both sides.

The Koreans in the south who suffered the most from the brutal North Korean assault have not forgotten that it was the Americans who responded immediately to the unprovoked attack, supporting an out-numbered, out-gunned South Korea with ground, sea and air forces.

North Korea's Kim Il-Sung has not forgotten that it was this American intervention, supported by other U.N. forces, that thwarted the plan that he had developed with his mentor, Joseph Stalin, for the rapid annexation of South Korea into the Communist Empire. The continuous forty-year presence of significant numbers of U.S. combat forces on the Korean Peninsula has served as an effective antidote to any amnesia on the part of Kim Il-Sung on this subject.

China's Mao Tze-tung never forgot the terrible devastation inflicted upon his military forces by American field artillery and close support aircraft when the North Vietnamese urged him to intervene on their behalf during the Vietnam conflict.

The military commanders of the People's Republic of China were awed by the speed and accuracy with which U.S. artillery and air could be massed on them and the ability of the American logisticians to keep the guns and aircraft supplied with incredible quantities of ammunition and ordnance. The Chinese elected to provide their socialist brethren in Vietnam with advice and support from the sanctuary of China itself.

And perhaps most important, the collective and individual leaders who replaced Joseph Stalin in the Former Soviet Union have not forgotten the lessons of the Korean War. Even before the death of Stalin, who was personally involved with the planning and conduct of the Korean War, the Soviet Armed Forces discovered a shocking fact which they have never before revealed but have not forgotten. When the best Russian pilots were flying their MIG-15's against the U.S. Air Force F-86 pilots, they lost approximately 9 Russian to every F-86 shot down. Our pilots believed that they were fighting Russian-trained Koreans when in fact they were flying against the Soviet 64th Interceptor Aviation Corps consisting of three Aviation Divisions and two Anti-Aircraft Artillery Divisions. The Anti-Aircraft Artillery Divisions remained in North Korea throughout the conflict but the Aviation Divisions were forced to operate from the sanctuary of Chinese territory north of the Yalu River.

Those of you who fought the air war over Korea have additional reasons to be proud. You were not fighting against a newly created third-world air force; you were fighting the first team, the very finest, combat-tested heroes of the second world war. You inflicted such unacceptably high casualties on the Soviet Air Force that Moscow sent a commission headed by two senior general officers to investigate. The Commander of the 64th Interceptor Aviation Corps, General Lobov, was relieved of his command due to the superior airmanship of the 5th Air Force pilots.

There can be no question that the positive effect of that lesson of the Korean War on the long term deterrent value of NATO, with its large commitment of conventional U.S. Army and Air Force units. In fact, if it had not been for the Korean War in which the United States demonstrated its national will to exercise military power, and the awesome effectiveness of that power across land, sea and air, the combined Chinese and Soviet Empires would likely have continued their expansion of neighboring countries through military aggression.

As more of the secret files of the former Soviet union are revealed, we find ourselves reaching new conclusions about the successes and failures of our national policies during and immediately following the Korean War. We have mentioned some of them The aggressors were shocked at the speed with which President Truman decided to intervene, the effectiveness of our mobilization and movement of military forces to the Korean Peninsula, and the powerful way in which the United nations was galvanized into action against them.

The Soviet union changed its national strategy to achieve its consistent goal of world domination. The strategy went from "hot to cold war;" from overt aggressor to covert, unconventional conflict; from defense against our strategic bombers to the development of a force of Intercontinental Ballistic Missiles capable of delivering a devastating first strike against the major cities of the United States; and finally, they changed their propaganda and psychological efforts to discredit the power of the U.S. Military to a theme of destroying the will of the national leaders to use U.S. military power.

Approximately 12 years ago the United States started two significant changes in national security policy. In the first case, President Ronald Reagan announced that the

United States was going to shift away from the policy of Mutual Assured Destruction, which was really a policy of revenge rather than defense. The President announced that we were going to establish a space-based ballistic missile defense system to defend this country rather than rely on the threat of retaliation as the only means of deterrence. He authorized the Strategic Defense Initiative Office to develop and test the weapon systems recommended by the High Frontier Project, headed by General Daniel O. Graham.

The activation of the Strategic Defense Initiative Office produced an incredible reaction from the Soviet Union, whose military commanders expressed the great fear that this technological end-run would emasculate their formidable strategic rocket force. The pressure on Gorbachev was increasing from inside his own government. Gorbachev remonstrated and threatened at the Reykjavik Summit Meeting, but President Reagan stood firm.

The second major change in our national security policy, which really pulled the linch pin from the Soviet apple cart, was the decision by President Reagan to provide assistance to those victims inside the Soviet Empire who where willing to fight for their freedom, in addition to those threatened peoples on the outside who wished to remain free. For over forty years our policy had been to contain the Soviet union and to provide internal defense security assistance to those threatened by the Soviets.

The Reagan Doctrine acknowledged that the Captive Nations were our greatest allies and deserved our encouragement and support in their aspirations for freedom. The provision of subtle but effective assistance to the Polish, Afghan, Nicaraguan, Angolan and other freedom fighters around the world gave hope and encouragement to all enslaved peoples everywhere and rekindled the fires of nationalism, religion, free enterprise and individual rights. The internal pressures generated by these expanding aspirations inside the Soviet Bloc very quickly fractured, then completely fragmented, the Soviet Monolith. As the world watched on TV, its most powerful leader fell in disgrace and such core symbols of Communism as the Berlin wall and the statues of Lenin crashed to the ground amid clouds of dust and shouts of joy.

Today, as we commemorate the 40th Anniversary of the official end of the war in Korea, we as veterans of that conflict can stand tall with pride, knowing that our efforts placed the first hairline cracks in the foundations of Communism. As close as we were at the time, we could not see them, but they were there, and they were growing.

Only now have we been able to speak with the Soviet and Chinese commanders, staff officers, advisors and participants on the north Korean side of the conflict. The more we learn, the more we realize that the victory that seemed to escape us in one nation in 1953 was in fact lying hidden in the now fatally damaged foundations upon which the communist empires sought to build. It was only years later, when the communist policies and programs were set in concrete, that the devastating effects of these cracks were so dramatically felt. The victorious battles waged by American and U.N. troops were not, in fact forgotten.

It is difficult to discuss this delayed victory over Communism with my friends in South Korea, in view of the fact that Kim Il-Sung remains in power across the DMZ, and is frantically engaged in the development of nuclear weapons and the acquisition of missiles to deliver them. He is no less irrational than he was in 1950 when he assumed that the United States had little interest in the Korean Peninsula and would be unlikely to react to his ill-conceived adventure to the south. He remains a dedicated communist to this day. [Since deceased! publisher's note]

As a result of President Clinton's recent trip to the Republic of Korea, there can be no confusion about U.S. policies towards Korea. The President made three points:

1. **If North Korea uses, or attempts to use, a nuclear weapon against anyone, North Korea will be "rubbleized."**

2. **If the Republic of Korea is threatened by an attack from the north, the U.S. will respond regardless of whether or not it is currently engaged in a conflict elsewhere.**

3. **The ROK will be included as a key player along with the United States in maintaining stability in the entire Western Pacific area.**

With his economy in shambles, and his Russian and Chinese allies now on good terms with a robust and prosperous South Korea, the options open to Kim Il-Sung are rapidly diminishing. The military option has now lost its attractiveness. If he is smart, his son, Kim Jong-Il will seek a "German Solution" and call for a form of unification that will save his people from starvation or worse.

The realities of the German Experience, however, suggest to the South Koreans that they would prefer that the communists be given a few years of economic recovery under some form of capitalism before they become fully responsible for the totally bankrupt North Korean society.

While a unified Korea is not yet a reality, it will most surely come in our lifetimes. When this happens, we veterans of the Korean War will have a great cause for celebration and personal pride. As my dear friend and mentor, General Richard G. Stilwell, once told a group of Korean War Veterans : "Stand tall in pride. You won big!"

I repeat to you today : **"Stand tall in pride. You won REAL big!"**

+++++

The CHALLENGE for FREEDOM

REMAINS in ASIA

by Luis A. Villa-Real
Brig. General, Republic of the Philippines

It is most unfortunate that as a consequence of the apparent collapse of communism and the end of the "Cold War", complacency has set in within the free world, which has mistakenly and with serious future consequences, concluded that all threats have disappeared and no longer exists. It is a simplistic assessment of a situation as volatile ass it is uncertain -- to say the least.

In the Asian-Pacific region, the tide of democratic reforms that have swept and transformed Eastern Europe, remained unwelcome to the totalitarian regimes in some Asian countries.

The impact of Soviet events on China, will take time to fully emerge. Progressives are greatly heartened and even more officials will adjust to the prevailing wind.

China's economic strength has increased rapidly in the past decade. Encouraging foreign trade, technology and investments has undoubtedly quickened the pace in the sector. These past few years, Taiwan capital has been heavily invested therein. talks between the two sides have been on-going and two-way visits have increased considerably.

Deng Xiaoping has claimed that the Chinese people now have the "broadest democracy that has ever existed in history". Certainly, twenty years of economic reforms have brought great changes. It is tempting to view the prosperity in China's coastal region as a sign that the old communist system is being swept rapidly away by free market and investments in the private sector. The idea that the communist regime will soon collapse as it apparently did in Eastern Europe and what was once the Soviet Union, has strong appeal, but it is doubtful it will happen. Communist regimes were swept away in Eastern Europe and the Soviet Union by economies that came to a halt. The communist party in China may be attempting to make it appear that it has abandoned Marxism, but it still commands the gun and manipulates economic progress by its own control of the levers of government. Frightened by, and scornful of the collapse of the Soviet Union, the leadership which crushed the Democracy Movement at Tiananmen more than five years ago and imprisoned those who created the "Democracy Wall" ten years before that, is all the more determined to hold on to power.

We have for a long time believed that political liberalization must precede or accompany economic liberalization. How then is China's astounding economic growth explained without the corresponding political liberalization? With the high GNP, the same disjunction between a dynamic economy and repressive Leninist political system that existed at the time of the 1989 Tiananmen massacre remains in being, but retains the potential to produce a similar but much greater social explosion in the future.

Will this economic upsurge continue after Deng Xiao ping fades from the scene? Here again, like in Russia and North Korea, their future after the present rulers pass out of the picture, is most uncertain and many changes are bound to develop.

A few years ago, the leaders of China openly proclaimed their claim, "by reason of history", to the entire South China Sea region. Therein lie the Paracels and the Spratleys. Such claim may be construed as a mere bluff or a serious assertion of sovereignty, ready to be exercised by military power, if need be.

Turning to the military dimension, we must look at its modernization. The Chinese have been trying to modernize for a long time. It was once more a question of modernizing a mind set and attitude toward technology than getting equipment. But now they have access to Russian technology and they are buying a fair amount. While it is not the most sophisticated, it is solid, medium-level technology the Chinese can use.

The Chinese are putting new investment into their three million strong standing armed forces. They have acquired the capability for air refueling and have constructed a 2600 meter long landing field on Woodland Island (Paracels?) which can handle their heaviest aircraft. They have expanded their navy, providing it a power projection capability reaching as far as the Spratleys.

Their vigorous arms sales program which is increasing in sophistication includes exports of their M-11 missile and other weapons. They continue to, one way or another, transfer nuclear technology to countries like Iran and Pakistan, notwithstanding U.S. efforts for the last five years, to get commitments to stop such transfers.

As recently as last October 7, China continued testing a new generation of ballistic missile warheads by exploding an underground nuclear device at its far western desert site at Lop Nor. It was the third such blast in the past two years. She is likewise testing her miniaturization program and continues to develop her second-generation ballistic missiles. While the new warheads are smaller than China's older ones, they are more powerful in explosive yield.

With the military controlling arms exports, it can be assumed the new weapons are on the shopping lists of Third World terrorist regimes.

With the on-going developments above described, as well as on satellite guided anti-ship missiles and surveillance sensors high in space, we can expect a highly modernized Chinese force in the early 21st Century, with a powerful offensive capability.

Early February this year, a tower with protruding antennas was observed in one of the islands of the Spratleys, within Philippine territory. The station was apparently manned by personnel in uniform, moving around the premises. Several naval vessels and fishing boats, later identified as Chinese, were likewise observed in the sea around the island. Chinese sources claimed this facility was to provide shelter for Chinese fishermen in emergencies.

This exercise could possibly be to test the reactions of the **United States, japan, South Korea, The Republic of China on Taiwan and the members of ASEAN.** The three highly industrialized countries of Northeast Asia which depend for raw materials almost entirely from external sources that must traverse the South China Sea area claimed by China, would be the most seriously affected in the event she uses force to impose her claim and controls the area.

It is obvious the move was planned and executed so as not to provoke any violent reactions by the affected countries, which may lead to serious consequences prematurely - that may expose and derail future plans.

This may be but a preview of what to expect in our region in the foreseeable future.

We therefore face **a China that cannot be ignored as important as she is - with the world's largest population, nuclear weapons, a permanent seat in the United Nations Security Council, a potentially huge market and a rich civilization. It launches satellites and sells missiles and other armaments. It is prominent in regional issues as Indochina and Korea and in global issues as environment and drugs. No one should think of isolating her. If the political decentralization and carefully limited liberalization continues, China will be an increasingly significant power in the future, worrisome to many of her neighbors.**

In Vietnam, we have a situation where her rulers, faced with the appalling revelations of the failure of communism, have two options: They may lay the blame for failure at the feet of other followers of Marx rather than at the failure of his doctrines. They are still believes in the ultimate victory of Marx, Lenin and Ho Chi Minh. Although those ideas have caused untold misery to millions and have totally failed, they are looking for a path to a better future for a hungry Vietnam crippled with inefficiency and corruption. It is encouraging and receiving foreign investments and U.S. assistance, perhaps because she has opted for a liberal democratic system.

The end of the cold war has not had any effect on **North Korea.** Her membership in the United Nations together with South Korea still leaves her with few friends and many disadvantages. She has previously resisted membership and has consistently opposed cooperation on the international stage.

Korea's traditional importance in Northeast Asia, has been that of a land bridge connection the Asian mainland with the Japanese Islands and the Pacific Ocean. North Korea adjoins Russia and is an excellent strategic location from which to expand Russian interests in the region. for over fifty years she has been a strategic buffer for the former Soviet Union in the Far Ease. After German unification and the liquidation of the Warsaw pact, what could the Russian government's relation with North Korea be today?

The strategic importance of the Korean peninsula to Russian interests cannot be overemphasized, regardless of the type of government running the country. She has to play a key role in that part of the world, to only because of the region's strategic importance to her, **but to lend substance and meaning to her being a part of Asia. This reality must be accepted by all.**

The passing of Kim Il Sung and the transition to his son, Kim Jong-Il has temporarily relieved the tension created by North Korea's intransigence in fully opening up her nuclear facilities to inspections by the United Nations notwithstanding former President Carter's visit to that country for that purpose.

What are the present and future relations between and among Russia, now in transition, China with her economic and military build up, Vietnam adopting a liberal democratic system and the succession of Kim Jong-Il to his father in North Korea --- not forgetting Genghis Khan's route of conquest to Europe from Mongolia through Russia and the withdrawal of his forces back to Russia where they remained for two hundred years in the early 11th Century. Napoleon and Hitler both tried to conquer Russia from the West with both attempts ending in disaster for both of them

With Eastern Europe free and struggling in its transition, Latin America successfully pursuing the enshrined ideals of freedom and democracy, leaving only Cuba in isolation, we focus our attention on the changing geo-political complexions in **Mainland China, Northeast and Southeast Asia.**

1 March 1995

+++++

An Appeal to the

U.S. LEAGUE

FOR FREEDOM & DEMOCRACY

by Mike Huckabee
Governor of the State of Arkansas

The U.S. League for freedom and Democracy has re chartered itself in order to become a growing voice for the principles of human rights and personal liberty throughout the world. In recognizing the frantic pace at which our world is changing politically and culturally, we have felt that it's important to form a new organization whose goals mirror those of the World League, but yet an organization which recognizes that a bonafide U.S. chapter needs to reflect an old fashioned view of freedom by the employment of new fashioned methods.

We see two of our most important tasks as being inspiration and education. Many American students have little or no knowledge of or appreciation of their own heritage of freedom and democracy. The current trends in the United States seems more bent on how students "feel" about life than what they actually know about life!

We recognize that we must inspire before we can inform. Modern day stories of courage from across the world of the struggle for freedom will hopefully inspire a quest for understanding how our own nation is indeed the result of suffering, service and sacrifice.

Through videos, school curriculum supplements and assembly programs, as well as world class conferences throughout the nation, we hope to bring the message of freedom and democracy to those young citizens whose lives and leadership are crucial to our continuance.

Good citizenship is impossible without an appreciation of how each person's responsible behavior contributes to the overall climate of the larger community of local, state or national government. Freedom and personal rights cannot exist in a vacuum, but must function within the context of shared responsibility. sadly, the emphasis of the past thirty years in America has been upon individual rights to such an exclusive degree, that an entire generation is taking the reins of leadership without a proper understanding of corporate responsibility.

The U.S. LEAGUE hopes to become a voice for the values that have shaped the growth periods in America, and to foster a new appreciation for the role of a strong national defense in maintaining peace here and abroad.

In the so-called "post cold war period," far too many national leaders believe that the need for a ready and strong military is on the wane. Without advocacy for the importance of cutting edge technology and readiness, we could in a very short time find ourselves vulnerable to the demands of an otherwise weak opponent in the context of an international crisis. Downsizing should not and must not mean "downgrading," and the League offers a vital platform from which to counter the claims of those who would increase domestic social spending at the expense of a nation which still has the capacity to defend itself with the weaponry which we manufacture for ourselves.

By keeping our young, but ambitions organization clearly focused and striving for the input of other like minded lovers of freedom and democracy, we stand to see significant gains in membership and participation at our conferences. We further believe that we will be able to begin aggressively developing an outreach to student leadership organizations to begin equipping tomorrow's leaders with an insight into their heritage and freedom.

One of our most challenging tasks is raising the necessary funds crucial to the launch of the effort. The most novice of physics students realize that more energy is required to start movement from a dead stop than to maintain an already moving object. Indeed, more funds are needed to start the movement of a reawakened appreciation of freedom and democracy than will be needed to maintain its speed once fully operational.

Every effort will be made, and the mood is optimistic among Board members, towards securing the funds, and bringing the U.S. LEAGUE forward to challenge a new generation of Americans to savor the benefits derived from living as free citizens, and to serve as ambassadors for freedom to peoples around the world.

+++++

The GOALS of the U.S. LEAGUE

FOR FREEDOM & DEMOCRACY

Victor T. H. Tsuan, Ph.D.

In the western world, freedom and democracy are part of our most cherished and enduring heritage. As the world becomes ever more interdependent and inter-related, cross cultural understanding will become ever more important. From a study of the rise and fall of Communist, Fascist and Nazi movements in the twentieth century, one can detect the patterns of thought and action shaping present-day trends and the direction in which they are heading.

The reason why the United States id commonly respected by the majority of people all over the world is that it is full of humanitarian spirit, equal opportunity and respect for the good and honest nature of mankind. for instance, when famine struck Russia in 1921, Herbert Hoover took the lead in organizing relief. The United States Congress allocated $4 million of surplus Army medical supplies to the Red Cross for relief to the Russians. Recently at the beginning of the Operation Restore Hope in Somalia, American troops were greeted by cheering Somali crowds, who carried with them the hope of a world appalled by anarchy and famine.

At present, violence in every form, seems to be increasing at Bosnia and Herzegovina, Palestine, South Africa, Mainland China, Cuba, Haiti, Vietnam, Cambodia, Rwanda and Myanmar. Their people are living amid political and social turmoil, economic hardship and fear of mass murder. What is alarming is that almost one third of mankind lives under some form of totalitarianism, enslaved and unable to free themselves. unless the course of history be changed, these unfortunate people will loose their human qualities and remain simply tools of their slave masters, often without even being aware of it. Retaining communication and maintaining aid, if feasible, to those people is most essential. Without such supportive contact, they could easily have their faith and hope destroyed, and even loose the will to survive and will not have the ability to discern good from evil. These nations are unhappy remnants of the cold war which has become a symbol of the Administration's failure and frustrations in international affair. Instead of responding to individual crisis as they arise, the U.S. League for Freedom and Democracy advocates the eliminating mis-perceptions of various cultures and undertakes a sustained initiative to transform the undemocratic countries into a far more effective instrument for safeguarding democracy and human rights.

The League is a non-profit organization and relies on voluntary contributions from individuals, organizations, corporations and foundations for it's support.

The purpose of the U.S. League is to capture the spirit of our age. The major emphasis is to promote world peace and freedom with a maximum justice for all people and the preservation of human rights and dignity under a democratic form of government. We pledge to follow the goals as outlined below :

First. We urge people of good will to share the American democratic ideas and basic human values that can be communicated effectively by working together and to build strong foundations for permanent world peace with resorting to violence.

Second. To deal with immediate as well as long raange solutions to such critical issues as failing international economies, national self-determination, social and cultural envionment, univesal human rights, population growth, refugee, hunger, poverty, and all forms of totalitarianism, especially communism.

Third. To urge the younger generation to realize that humanity renews and continues itself. It is our goal to transmit the inherited wisdom and insights of our traditional values which is stronger than we think, such belief in the existence of a Supreme Creator, the ultimate source of all being and goodness in the Universe; compassion and harmony; lofe and regard for all rfellow beings.

Fourth. To promote the rights of all peoples of the world to live, develop and prosper politically, culturally and economically in independent sovereign nations, under freely elected political and socio-economic systems, with governments of, by, and for the nation's people.

Finally, during the post World War II era, America has made almost unbelieveable material and social progress. The rapid advance in scientific and technological fields of knowledge has produced nuclear energy and astronauts have set foot on the moon. We must convince the people of the world of the American good intentions to lead the world towards democratic freedom.

The collapse of the Soviet Communism does not guarantee the permanent, universal triumph of freedom and democracy. We resolutely affirm our commitment and determination to pursue these goals in unity for freedom and democracy of all nations. We must consciously and actively determine in advance what kind of future we want. In the days to come, we may be facing a long dark night. But we are convinced that with conviction and confidence, the light of ultimate victory of the common goals shared by manking shall some day come, and then we will rejoice.

+++++

Chapter VI

SCENIC CHINA

TSINGTAU, CHINA; 1914

As Experienced by a German Aviator

by Robert E. Whittaker

A few excerpts from the 1994 non-fiction book DRAGON MASTER; The Kaiser's One-Man Air Force in Tsingtau, China, 1914.

The author was born in Shanghai and lived in China and Tsingtau for over 17 years and heard accounts of the siege from former German soldiers. His father, the late Edward G. Whittaker was a former President of the Shanghai Tiffin Club; 1963-64.

Over 3,000 pages of historical documents, photographs and microfilm from the archives of five nations including accounts and letters from "Old China Hands," were acquired to create this unique book that took over three years to complete.

During the first 3 months of World War I the German Naval base of Tsingtau (German spelling) (or Tsingtao, now Qingdao) was besieged by superior Japanese and (token) British land-sea-air forces. In all there were some 60,000 against 4500 Germans of which only 4000 were proficient to fight...nearly a fifteen to one ratio.

This was the first time in history that a combination of land, sea and air forces was used during a campaign. It was the military "laboratory" that tested every known state-of-the-art weapon (except chemical) and awakened the sleeping monster of Japan's 20th Century militarism.

Woven within this literary tapestry are the sights, smells, sounds and suffering of China over 80 years ago as it was occupied by "FOREIGN DEVILS" from three warring nations... Germany, England and Japan.

Tsingtau is noteworthy for several reasons. It has been under six flags; Manchu, Imperial Germany, Japanese / British, Republic of China and since 1949, the People's Republic of China.

It was one of the ten most beautiful port cities in the world as claimed, during the 1930's, by Fitzpatrick the documentary film producer of the theater series "Traveltalk." It was the cleanest, most modern and healthful city in the Far East.

Until 1891 Tsingtau had no history. At that time the Imperial Chinese Government decided that Kiaochow Bay was a strategic part of the Shantung coast and established a garrison of a few thousand men there. The fishing village was named Tsing-tau (Ching-Dao) "Green Island" after it's namesake in the bay.

In 1897 two German missionaries were murdered in the interior of Shantung Province. Whether this was perpetrated by political dissidents, bandits or religious fanatics was never determined.

The Germans welcomed the excuse to thwart the British colonial expansion in China which had previously acquired Hong Kong in the south and Wei-Hai-Wei on the Shantung north coast. In typical gunboat diplomacy of the times, but with utmost swiftness, the German Emperor, Wilhelm dispatched Admiral Otto von Diedrichs with three German warships, the _Comoran_, the _Princess Wilhelmine_ and the flagship _Kaiser._ On November 13, 1897 they steamed into the bay, fired a few shots at the Yamen (police station), landed a contingent of 600 marines, ran up the German ensign and as the ship's cannon gave a twenty-one gun salute, took possession of the village. The few Chinese troops fled. There was no bloodshed.

In March 1898, the Manchu government in Peking had no other choice but sign a treaty, leasing Tsingtau and a district around it of some 500 square kilometers together with the deep-water bay of Kiaochow and the islands off the coast to Imperial Germany. The term of the lease was 99 years; the purpose, "for the repairing and equipping ships; for storing of materials and supplies for the same and for all other furnishings belonging thereto."

The treaty also authorized the construction of a railway, granted concessions for mining within a thirty li (nine mile) zone along the railway and provided for the establishment of fortifications for "the protection of the harbor."

In March 1904 the harbor was completed. On the circular mole surrounding it were workshops accommodating 2,000 men. All types of ship repairs were possible and small steamers could be built and lifted by an enormous 160 ton crane. There was also a 16,000 ton floating dry dock installed, the largest in Asia, one of the largest and finest in the world. On June 1, 1904 the 395 kilometer railway between Tsingtau and Tsinanfu was open to traffic operated for the most part by the Germans.

The former fishing village was soon transformed into a modern commercial port and naval bastion by the influx of the German navy, marines and civilian colonists. Their engineers laid out the city according to the most current European designs of the early Twentieth century. They literally built the city from "scratch."

They began with a modern sewer and water system to guarantee Tsingtau the healthiest conditions in all of Asia. Under German supervision, thousands of Chinese coolies constructed wide macadamized streets, tree-lined promenades and set up an excellent electrical system. The brick, stone and red slate-roofed buildings, schools, churches, hospitals, hotels, residences, beer gardens and cafes, including a fine German brewery, looked like miniature transplants of the "Fatherland."

Hundreds of thousands of traditional German trees; pine, oak, beech, alders and birch were imported from Europe and carefully planted. The acacia trees, from German

East Africa bearing large sharp thorns, were especially useful to camouflage and protect the fortifications. They also grew rapidly and in late Spring would blossom into heavy grape-like clusters of sweet white flowers that produced an excellent honey. The flowers could also be boiled and used to sweeten food and cereal.

In mid-summer of 1914 over 100 new houses and buildings were under construction. The colonial Germans provided a constant proof of their industriousness. With Tsingtau as their headquarters, the mining companies, banking firms, railroad engineers, merchants and businessmen spread throughout north China even to the Russian border. The British influence while strong in Hong Kong and south China was being reduced up north by the Germans. At that time only two strong powers were in the area; Japan and Germany.

The spectacular Japanese victory over the Russians had amazed the European powers including the United States. The latter had no further aspirations of colonial footholds in Asia, after acquiring Guam and the Philippines from Spain in 1898, annexing Hawaii and acquiring a portion of Samoa. Instead America came into the Pacific as a "benevolent colonist" and to the Far East as a business trading power. Concurrently the American diplomats began extolling their "Open Door" policy. They wanted equal trade and access opportunities for everyone in China rather than a division of the country into national colonies and spheres of influence. Somehow China's territorial sovereignty, no matter how carefully papered over, must be protected for the economic profits of everyone.

Europeans, after witnessing the United States grabbing territory at a record rate, were not totally convinced about these proposals. With the exception of Russia, they eventually agreed to the principle of the American position, but none gave a sincere commitment. They accepted the idea as long as it cost them nothing. Besides, they needed time to further their own aspirations.

The most serious of these ambitions centered in St. Petersburg. In the aftermath of the Boxer rebellion in 1900, the Russians absorbed even more of Manchuria and completed their general take-over of the entire area. They obviously planned for an indefinite stay, posing an immediate military threat to Japan and China.

Japan countered by launching hostilities against Russia in 1904. The humiliating defeat of Russia a year later and Japan's challenging role was now igniting both nationalism and militarism in Asia.

In 1911 the Ching Dynasty of the Manchus, said to be "like a decayed log riddled by termites and covered with a rich gold brocade," crumbled before the Chinese Nationalists who were motivated by the ideals and writings of Dr. Sun Yat-sen.

To curry favor with the new Republic, Imperial Germany paid a considerable "cumshaw" to General Yuan Shi-kai who became the strong-man of China. The Germans, despite their somewhat tardy arrival in China, had developed a fine economic foundation for future growth and a powerful military bastion in Tsingtau.

CHAPTER 2 BEGINS AS THE GERMAN AVIATOR GUNTHER PLÜSCHOW ENDS HIS 6,600 TRANS-SIBERIAN TRAIN TRIP FROM BERLIN TO TSINGTAU.

The secondary train depot was in Tapautau, the Chinese quarter adjacent to Tsingtau that bordered the native junk harbor. The train would only stop here for a few moments to disconnect and let off the second and third class passengers. These were mostly Chinese peasants and coolie workers.

The Chinese shops that Plüschow could see from the train were a combination of east and west. Open to the sidewalk they exhibited a strange alfresco style of shopping. The main food market, was merely small shops grouped together under a single roof and provided a unique diversity of sights, sounds and smells.

Glazed duck and other prepared fowl hung by their necks and feet along with dried fish of many varieties. Large coffin-like troughs contained live fish to be chosen by the shopper. Pigs and chickens noisily objected to their cramped wicker baskets. Nondescript pieces of meat buzzing with flies were displayed in the racks of the butcher stores. The better butchers, who catered to Europeans, kept both the meat and the flies under glass.

Colorful vegetables and fruit and grain were in great abundance. The bakeries were filled with both Chinese unleavened "mantou" and various European breads and pastries. North China doesn't grow rice so more grain and noodles are eaten. Shoppers were Chinese as well as Europeans with their servants. Open touring automobiles were parked nearby and chauffeurs swapped gossip.

The train started again and slowly moved to the main station only a kilometer distant. Here the stores looked more European. The Chinese characters designating the name of the shop would be supplemented with a German hand-scripted caption, usually quite incongruous, possibly made up by a German with a curious sense of humor. A cobbler was named Mist Schuster, "Manure Boot-maker": And the shoe store next to him was "Manure no. 2." The barber was Schaum-Kopf, "Bubble-head;" A tailor was "Rooster" because of his raucous laughter. And so it went, a strange, yet humorous mingling of the east and west, a piece of Europe....a Teutonic foothold built here in China through the organized design and determined effort of the Germans.

CHAPTER 4; excerpts

The Navy aviator Leutnant (Lieutenant) Plüschow had been diligently fixing possible navigational points on his chart as they made their automobile tour of survey and inspection, escorted by the intelligence officer from the General Staff. Now the Oberleutnant wanted to drive to the base of Prinz Heinrich a 364 meter high mountain some 6 kilometers from the outer defenses. Pluschow had flown over this 1200 foot strategic site and in his subsequent report, questioned why there was no observation post situated here. He observed candidly that the location would be far better for directing German gun-fire than the near useless vulnerable captive balloon, the "Yellow Sausage." He received a slight rebuke for his choice of words in an official written report, but also praise for his suggestion.

Driving east on the dirt road along the coast they stopped in a tiny village at the base of Prinz Heinrich-berg. The open land sloped sharply upwards, scored by vertical ravines to where abruptly jagged rocks towered into the sky. One would have to be a mountain climber to reach the summit. The intelligence officer had said, that based on Pluschow's report, there was going to be an observations post located here. The officer scanned the mountain with his field glasses and compared it to a Takahashi postcard of the mountain. There was a definite difference. The photo had been altered. The only accessible way to the top had apparently been purposely deleted by the Japanese postcard photographer.

Takahashi was a Tsingtau institution. The Japanese spoke several languages and was renowned for his humor and knowledge of German and Western cultural ethics and customs. His good will and toothy smiling friendliness was irresistible. His photographs were of the highest state-of-the-art and his quality picture postcards of the area made superb souvenirs. There were few restrictions controlling his movements or photography.

Even the German Navy Captain, Meyer-Waldeck had commissioned Takahashi to take the official pictures when he became Governor of Tsingtau in 1911. Meyer-Waldeck's imposing height of 1.95 meters (6 foot 5 inches) was in sharp contrast to the very short stocky photographer. But unbeknownst to the Germans at that time, he was also a Japanese spy.

While the Oberleutnant was busy with his tripod mounted camera assisted by the petty officer, Plüschow had time to view the scenery, this time from the ground.

The mud and straw huts within the village were vastly different from Tsingtau and even the Chinese villages nearer the city. This was the real China, provincial and peaceful. While not far away the frantic preparations for the inevitable Japanese naval blockade and land siege made Tsingtau seem like a giant ant hill gone mad.

Curious children stopped their play of shuttle-cock and cat's cradle to gaze at the foreigners. Two men, with wisps of white facial hair growing out of moles, sat on small stools in the sun warming their old bones. Each had a song bird within individual bamboo cages with a piece of cuttle-fish bone stuck in it for bill sharpening. They sucked tiny pinches of strong black tobacco in bamboo pipes with brass bowls and stretched their necks to gawk. Two fishermen were launching their heavy sampan by picking up one end at a time suspended from a pole and revolving it end-for-end down the beach into the water.

Smells assailed Plüschow's nostrils; the garlicky odor of unwashed bodies; urine in the gutters; whiffs of hot rancid peanut oil from a food hawker's walking kitchen; rotting fish remains along a creek bank and refuse composting in pig pens. The smell of the Yellow Sea mingled with the overpowering stench of human and animal fertilizer spread on the fields by Shantung farmers who for generations have wrested a meager living from the sterile patches of earth. These peasants, in a never-ending desperate effort, struggled to give back to the land the only thing they could afford that would nourish the soil for yet another growing season.

And there were sounds, some which were familiar to Plüschow, many not. There were the barking of wonk dogs challenging the strangers and howls as they were struck by stones thrown by small boys. Chickens cackled as they too were chased. And there was the "Aye-Ho Ah-Ho" chant of coolies moving a heavy load. A tinsmith, his shop hanging from a bamboo shoulder pole, walked along, letting the clanging of metal strips announce to anyone with leaky pots and broken pans that he was available with soldering iron and shears. A smoking charcoal brazier dangled from the rear. A tailor passed with bolts of cloth piled high on his back. He carried a primitive foot pedal sewing machine in one hand and the other twirled a small drum on a stick with a tassel that made the "bunga-bunga" sound of his profession. A blind man felt his way along a wall with a reed cane iron and shears. A smoking charcoal brazier dangled from the rear. A tailor passed with bolts of cloth piled high on his back. He carried a primitive foot pedal sewing machine in one hand and the other twirled a small drum on a stick with a tassel that made the "bunga-bunga" sound of his profession. A blind man felt his way along a wall with a reed cane and flicked his wrist so a tiny hammer on a leather thong struck a small gong. He also had a begging bowl suspended around his neck. The click of a stick on a hollow gourd told those behind walls that a monk was passing. It was good "joss" to drop a few coins into beggar bowls. Plüschow would need good luck. It was only days before the Japanese would attacked Tsingtau. He gave them each a copper cash.

Plüschow had met China, centuries old, unchanged.....but it would not be so for long.

POSTSCRIPT:

The lone German aviator, Lt. Gunther Plüschow was given the title "Dragon Master" by the Chinese because of the dragon tattoo on his left arm and his daring exploits flying a primitive Rumpler-Taube (Dove) monoplane against nine Japanese army and navy bi-planes. He is credited (unofficially) with shooting one down.

Plüschow survived the siege before Tsingtau surrendered on November 7, 1914 and escaped under orders to neutral China. He then escaped Chinese internment in Nanking, fled to Shanghai, and then to America aboard a U.S. ship. Leaving New York aboard an Italian ship with forged Swiss papers, the vessel was suspiciously diverted to Gibraltar where he was captured, but later made a daring escape from a British P.O.W. camp in England and July 4, 1915 he fled to Germany to become a decorated hero. However, this heroic pioneer aviator fell "through the cracks of history," until now.

+++++

V.I.P.'s
FOR THREE WEEKS
IN TAIWAN

June L. Aulick

The excitement began when my nephew, Lee Garnjost, and I walked down the ramp of the enormous Chiang Kai-Shek International airport outside of Taipei. Suddenly we heard our names called out in an unfamiliar accent.

The next minute Franklin Chen of the Tourism Bureau approached, relieved me of my carry-on bag, and guided us to the carousel where our luggage soon came whirling around. While Mr. Chen led us to an official who promptly examined our belongings I looked at the lines of tourists waiting to pass through customs. How lucky we were to receive this special attention!

The V.I.P treatment continued for the next three weeks as we toured the island province of the Republic of China from its northern tip down to Kenting National Park 250 miles to the south. We even had the thrill of driving up through the Sea of Clouds to Alishan for a spectacular view of the sun rising over Uyshan, the 13,114 foot peak formerly known as Mt. Morrison. All this extra special sightseeing was arranged by Lee's brother, John Garnjost, General Manager of an American firm based in Taipei.

"You've come just at the time when our company's annual outings are held." John explained as we made the 45-minute drive from the airport to his home, complete with swimming pool and patio in Yangmingshan. "Tomorrow we'll join about 60 members of the Consumer Division and see one of the latest show places in Taiwan, *Window on China*."

The next day we headed for the little town of Lungtan, 33 miles southwest of Taipei. With Franklin Wei, John's driver, at the wheel of his 2.8-liter Ford, we sped past rice and corn fields and lush green hills, kept verdant year round by plentiful rainfall. I understand why 16th century Portuguese mariners had called the island "Ilha Formosa." Beautiful Island.

A brief shower descended as we pulled up at the entrance to the Window of China exhibit which was opened in 1984 on four acres of ground. Tiny trains and boats moving toy-like tools along miniscule rails and waterways symbolized Taiwan's entry into the age of technology.

When the contingent from the office arrived, men and women both came forward and extended their hands in a friendly greeting. This gesture surprised me as I had heard that handshaking was not the custom in Taiwan. But here was example of the growing Western influence, along with the proliferation of McDonald's, doughnuts and ice cream.

The rain continued as we joined the cavalcade of buses and private cars enroute to Leofoo Safari Park. Opened in 1979 it covers 200 acres of ground, providing a home for more than 1,000 different species of animals. Soon after we turned into the entrance, an exuberant monkey jumped on the car, pounded on the roof, and, looking very disheveled from the rain, peered at us through the windshield.

From the Safari Park we proceeded up the mountainside along a winding road which led to Shihmen (Stone Gate) Dam. A multipurpose reservoir, it was designed to prevent floods and contribute to agriculture in the area.

We spent the night at the Shihmen Lake hotel, and arose at 6 A.M. the next morning for a hilarious game of "Gate Ball," (croquet to us). After a farewell ride around the lake, we started back to Taipei and stopped along the way at the mausoleum of General Chiang Kai-Shek who died in 1975.

The beautiful landscaped and immaculately tended sanctuary grounds were enclosed by lofty trees which afforded protection against the noise and distraction of the adjoining road. As we passed a tranquil pond where swans floated gracefully, Janice Nieh, John's secretary, informed us: "This land belonged to the General and he visited here often, but never really lived here. He chose this spot because it reminded him of this home on the mainland where he hoped eventually to be buried."

Inside, a picture of the first President of the R.O.C. hung above a mantle on which were placed candles and a bowl of fresh flowers. A white cross stood at the foot of the sarcophagus. We paused reverently for a few moments, bowing three times on direction from the presiding soldier.

Back in Taipei Saturday night we had dinner in the Pizza restaurant of the fabulous Lai Lai Sheraton hotel. The hotel lobby, with its circular, glass enclosed elevators topped with masses of flowers, looked like a scene from a fairy tale.

Sunday afternoon we attended the 4th of July celebration sponsored by the American Chamber of Commerce in the R.O.C. We watched teams of young men climbing and sliding in a greased pole contest, and then we settled down on the grass to enjoy the fireworks display. It concluded with a breathtaking horizontal waterfall of--- well it looked like a spreading curtain of sparklers. The evening wound up with a stroll through one of the crowded night markets where everything was on sale, from shoes to live shakes.

Accompanied by my two over-six-feet tall relatives, I felt safe among the slowly moving mass of strangers. I later learned that unescorted ladies going out at night in Taipei for dessert or just plain browsing have no need for alarm.

Our sightseeing in Taiwan included a trip to Hualien and a tour through the awe-inspiring Taroko Gorge. We got out of the bus to walk through the Tunnel of Nine Turns, hugging the rail as we gazed up at the three-thousand feet high marble cliffs around us, and down at the scary drop below where the river flowed whitely from fallen marble deposits.

In between jaunts, John invited me to conduct a writing seminar for members of his staff. At the end of the session he entertained us all at diner in the Executive Club's Majesty Hall atop the Lai Lai. At the end of the 12-course feast, Joseph Lin, head of the Employee relations Department, presented me with my very own name chop. A real thrill for this New Yorker!

EXOTIC HUANGSHAN

Samuel S. T. Chen, Ph.D.

Everybody knows that there is the Yellow River [Huang-ho] in China, but how many people have ever heard of the Yellow Mountain [Huangshan] there too? In fact, it is a range of mountains with spectacular views spreading over an area of more than 150 square kilometers [approximately 58 square miles] in Southeast China. It is situated in the heart of Anhui Province, about 650 miles south of Beijing [Peking] and 250 miles Southwest of Shanghai. Its esthetic charms have been admired and immortalized by generations of Chinese poets and painters, such as Li bai of the Tang Dynasty [618-906] and Shi-tao of the Qing Dynasty [1644-1912].

One of the reasons why Huangshan has been so obscure to most Westerners is probably its inaccessibility in the past. It was not open to foreigners until 1979. Now, with the completion of a new railroad between Nanjing [Nanking] and Nanchang, one can easily reach the mountain by taking an over-night sleeper in Shanghai or Nanjing and get off at Tunqi the next morning. There are air-conditioned buses connecting the Tunqi railroad station with the hotels at the foot of the Huangshan range. It is only a two hours' ride.

The hotel specially reserved for foreigners is called the Peach Brook Guest house [Taoyuan Binguan]. It is a Western-style multi-storeyed building with modest furnishings at reasonable prices. When a visitor arrives at the hotel, it is advisable to rest for a little while and do the preparation for mountain climbing. A pair of good walking shoes or sneakers, a walking staff or bamboo stick, and a light weight plastic raincoat are some of the necessities for any Huangshan climbers. Remember, not everyone is suitable for mountain climbing. Those with high blood pressure, asthma, heart disease or leg problems would be better off to stay in or around the hotel.

There are different way to climb the Huangshan. The toughest way is to face the mountain squarely and make a frontal attack. In this way, you will see the hundreds and hundreds of stone steps set into rugged cliffs at 45 to 80 degrees. To climb these steps is as exhausting as climbing the stairs of the Empire State Building in New York, and the mountain is much higher. The Empire State Building is only 741 feet high, while the Lotus Flower Peak of Huangshan is 1,873 meters or 6,147 feet above sea level.

A comparatively easier way is to go by the back of the mountain, because there are tour buses taking you to a point halfway up the mountain. From there you can proceed leisurely to the north Sea Guest house [Beihai Binguan] at the top of the mountain with many rest areas along the way. Some of the roadside pavilions and terraces will provide you with a close-up view of the various rocks, pines, flowers, waterfalls, pools, etc. Having thoroughly enjoyed the scenery at the summit, you can begin to descend the mountain by its front side. In order to get the maximum result, it is highly recommended that you take a break halfway and spend at least one night at the Jade Screen Hotel [Yuping Lou] , formerly known as Wenxuyuan. Here, at one glance, you can see three of the most famous peaks of Huangshan, namely, the Lotus flower Peak [Lianhua Feng], the Bright summit [Guangming Ding], and the heavenly Capital Peak [Tiandu feng]. As the saying goes: "Unless you come to Wenxuyuan, you haven't really seen the true face of Huangshan."

Finally, there is the easiest way to climb Huangshan, that is by riding the cable cars which were just completed recently. As a matter of fact, this is the only way for the elderly and handicapped to enjoy the beauty of Huangshan.

The characteristic attractions of Huangshan are generally classified into four categories: the fantastically shaped rocks, the swirling sea of clouds, the all-seasons hot springs, and the strange pines that grow on stones.

The beauty of the rocks of Huangshan lies not in their quality, which is granite in purple-brownish color, but in their shapes. Those rocks with proper names are just master-pieces of work of art skillfully sculptured by Mother Nature. For instance, the Xianren Qiru [Fairy Pointing the Way] is a rock standing up like a statue of Moses with his fingers pointing to the Red Sea. The Houzi Guanhai [Monkey Watching the Sea] vividly presents a profile of a monkey sitting on the beach of the sea. The Feilai Shi [Stone Coming by Flight] looks almost like the Washington Monument moved to China from Washington, D.C.

Because Huangshan has plenty of rainfall all year long, there is always a sea of clouds swirling around the peaks. On a sunny day, the clouds will reflect the sunshine in golden or silvery colors. If the clouds are driven by fast winds, the peaks emerging out of the clouds would give the impression of moving and dancing like floating boats in the sea. A spectacular view cherished by many tourists is to observe the ritual of watching sunrise in the early morning. It looks as if a ball of fire is burning out of a blanket of cotton without doing any damage. It is really wonderful!

Huangshan's pines are unusual, because they not only grow on fertile, but also cling to the face of stones. Their shapes vary. Most of the pines stand straight, but some of them are crooked and lying down. All of them have an even top like a crew-cut, and some of them have branches only on one side. The famous Yinkexum is a pine having branches stretching out to welcome the on-coming visitors with greeting hands. The Woulungxun, Fenghuangxun, and Heifuxun look exactly like a dragon. a phoenix, and a black panther respectively. There are altogether ten pines with proper names.

The famous hot springs of Huangshan are located some-where between the Purple Cloud Peak [Ziyin Feng] and the Peach Blossom Peak [Taohua Feng] at 630 meters [2,067 feet] above sea level. The water is fairly constant in temperature at 42 degrees C. [107 degrees F] throughout the year. Its volume changes little, regardless of dry seasons or wet seasons. Now, a bathhouse and a swimming pool have been built nearby for the public. Because the water contains sulfur, carbonate, and other minerals, it is believed that taking baths or swimming here would have therapeutic effects.

There are also many waterfalls and pools in Huangshan. The outstanding waterfalls are the Thousand-Foot Falls [Beichang Quan], the Man-Character-Shaped Falls

[Renzi Pao], the Nine-Dragon falls [Quilung Pao], and the most famous pools include the Blue Dragon Pool [Qinglung Tan], the White Dragon Pool [Bailung Tan], the Old Dragon Pool [Laolung Tan], and the Emerald Pool [Feicui Qi].

Besides, there are some rare species of animals, birds, and exotic plants in Huangshan, such as the golden-haired monkey, the silver pheasant, the musical Bayin bird, the heavenly-maiden flower, and the long-life Linzi fungus.

In conclusion, Huangshan has not only given inspiration to poets and painters, but also provided laboratory and proving ground for naturalists and scientists. It is a place not only for pleasure, but also for recreation, therapy, and other practical purposes. Certainly, it is worthy of every penny and effort to pay a visit.

+++++

"hsiang te i chang"

[The agreeable combination enhances the beauty]

Chapter VII

POETRY

THE HIMALAYAS ADVENTURE

Chien-Fu Kao

Spurring my horse through the driven snow,
Borne aloft by the blizzard I go.
High up on the icy summit stand I
Where earth meets the edge of sky.

Translated by Diana L. Kao

The above poem depicts Professor Chien-Fu Kao's Adventure in trying to climb on horseback up the Himalayas in 1943.

During this adventure, he encountered several severe snowstorms, felling him and his horse at times down the slope for hundreds of feet. As a result, he suffered an injury in his leg, and his eyes became almost blinded by the strong glaring sunlight on the Himalayas.

RANDOM THOUGHTS

Diana L. Kao

Cast a little bit of sunshine in a world of clouds,
Show a little bit of tolerance where hatred abounds.
Be gentle, kind, and understanding,
Urge to be harsh notwithstanding.
Peacefully together we live,
Cheerfully we try to give.
Let's make this world a pleasant one,
After all is said and done.

DANCING INK

David A. Heinlein

Wood and ink calligraphy
Clunk of scroll against the wall.
Gossamer thread writing---
Wind on jade.
Pu Ru's flying tails to his characters
Lin Yutang and hu Shih here
With a bird on a high branch.
Outside on Madison Avenue,
Interesting illegible graffiti
In red and black
On a white van.
The driver is Chinese.

KYOTO WEATHER

Rain pelts down.
Thunder roars from Shokokuji to Gosho.
Alixe opens the <u>shoji</u>
To see if it's hailing.

David A. Heinlein

THE TALISMAN

Swift water
Small smooth porcelain fragment,
Broken piece in the riverbed.
I pick it up,
Save it,
Savor it,
A Kyoto relic never sold.

David A. Heinlein

RAINY SEASON

At Matsugaoka,
Clouds heavy and wind strong
Lots of insects, birds.
Rain last night again.
Rain right now.

David A. Heinlein

VISIT to MAINLAND CHINA

Chinese men,
Smoking cigarettes,
Stand lost in thought
In front of
Lu Hsun's grave
In the Shanghai park.
Friendly eyes
Meet me
As I approach.

Bullet marks from Japanese strafing
Still visible
On the way to Sun Yat-   en's memorial.
Great press of people
Coming and going
At the entrance
Into the tomb.
Will there be a panic?
No. Patience.

Names of war dead
Inscribed on walls in Nanjing.
A monk lights two sticks of incense
In a Shanghai Zen temple.
They flare.

David A. Heinlein

POSTCARD FROM OTIS

I relax at our front porch table
In the kid's chair.
The calligraphy I painted
On the thick slab
Nine years ago
Leans against the wall.
Twice we've wood-lifed it.
It was beginning to rot
On the bottom
Under the arbor vitai,
So I brought it to the proch.

Dead leaves pile around it
In the corner.
I look at it every time
I go into the house.
Dust and grime from storms
Always cling through winter
out here: old screens,
old calligraphy, old house.

I've thought of selling
The calligraphy,
But Cecile didn't think
It was old enough yet.
Wood and white paint character
"POETRY" fade together.

The dirt and the age
don't bother me right now.
Just washed the cars,
Even wiped down my dash
And inner door frames,
Swept the front steps.

Those letters from Japan
Come less frequently,
But when they do,
They can still make me burn clean,
Like charcoal in a winter brazier
In a Kyoto house at Sanjo.

David A. Heinlein

IN SOUTHAMPTON

Ten Chinese vase deities
Tell birds what humans say.
They unlock voices, laughter
Sorrow
Tears.
The birds
Walk in muck
In Southampton
Where gnats bite.
The bird souns penetrate
My car, where, having fled
The bugs, I sit & watch & listen & write.
The sun has gone behind a huge thunderhead.
Chinese characters
Like the Drunkard
Or The Fool
Or The Idiot
Haunt my mind today.
The bird flies over the beach---
Rock-Drill.
The bird turns
Heads away out where I was.
I am the bird
That hears language from
Lafcadio Hern's death-place.
3 centuries open up.
The bird turns sharply.
My car a Japanese import
My head a Japanese-Chinese
   and yes American too invention
Sea water on face 50 minutes ago
Clean jeans
Bought in Japan---
I bought another 2 books in Southampton today
I walked another stretch of beach at Little Plains Road.

David A. Heinlein

A few "BERRIES " OF WISDOM
from the book "Strawberry Wisdom" by
Lao Wei

To know how little one knows
is to have genuine knowledge.

Not to know how little one knows
is to be deluded and foolish.

The wise man is not deluded,
because he knows and accepts
his ignorance as ignorance,
and thereby has genuine knowledge.

Lao Tzu
6th Century B. C.

Those born with an under-
standing of the Universe
belongs to the highest
type of humanity.

Those who understand it
as the result of study . . .
come *second*.

Those who study it
with great difficulty . . .
come *third*.

And the people who
find it too difficult
to attempt study . . .
come *last*.

Confucius
551-479 B.C.

It is said that a true Master
is known . . . not by the number
of his disciples . . . but whether
his disciples become Masters
themselves!

Anonymous

He who worries over little things
Is of little mentality.

He who worries over BIG things
Is of bigger mentality.

He who worries over NOTHING
Is of an enlightened mentality.

Lao Wei

To know is to know
that to know . . .
is not to know.

Confucius
551-479 B.C.

He who walks
in the foot prints
of others. . .
. . .BECAUSE IT IS EASIER. . .
will never leave
his own tracks
in the snows of life.

Lao Wei

A Man. . .
a Woman . . .
a Family . . .
a Village . . .
a City . . .
a Nation . . .
a World . . .
Should be like a grove
of bamboo.
Each standing separately,
yet, with roots inter-twined . . .
with leaves gently caressing
one another.

Lao Wei

OLD SHANGHAI

Shanghai.......The name brings to the eye...a phantom city.
Lanterns glowing red, dark streets, blue gowns and....
Dimly overhead....the up-turned roofs near touching.
Opium dens and gambling houses; sing-song girls and tiny feet;
Black queues, gaunt hands, a beggars whine.....
A kaleidoscope of faces in the streets.

But suddenly before your eyes the real city lies.
A strange crude mingling of the East and West.
Stores stocked with everything of Europes' best.
Tall buildings hemming in the steady flow
Of rickshaw, tram and motor....yet, but a coppers' toss
From off the tramlines you may find with ease
The teeming struggling life of the Chinese.

A piece of Europe dropped here by mistake,
A restless Western, bidding China..."Wake!"
A medley city, full of life and sin,
A brilliant nervous Cosmopolitan.
Full of the subtle cunning of the East,
Yet openhanded, loving sport and feast.
A wild, gay, high-strung, hustling, vivid town,
Shanghai..........chief jewel in China's crown.

"An Old China Hand"

Chapter VIII

MISCELLANEOUS

TEA and ASHES

by

Irene Corbally Kuhn

PRECEDE

American world traveler, newspaper correspondent, radio broadcaster and magazine writer **Irene Corbally Kuhn** lived and worked in Shanghai as a young reporter for the *China Press* newspaper in the 1920's. Following the death of her husband Bert L. Kuhn, she returned with their two-year-old daughter, Rene, to the United States.

Subsequent assignments took her around the globe. As World II was ending, in the spring of 1945, she flew over "the Hump" from India to China where she managed to broadcast the first reports to the United States, in August, from liberated Shanghai via a U.S. Seventh Fleet communications ship anchored in the Whangpoo River.

Irene Corbally Kuhn, a longtime member of the Shanghai *Tiffin* Club of New York , died on December 30, 1995, two weeks before her 98th birthday. She was in a home in Concord, Massachusetts where she had lived for the past year, near her daughter, Rene [Mrs. Douglas] Bryant, her granddaughter Heather [Mrs. John] Jordan, and her great-grandchildren, twins Phoebe and Douglas, born in January 1994.

Editor's Precede by Elinor P. Griest

TEA & ASHES

The Customs clock banged out seven long strokes. I came awake reluctantly. I had been up until nearly 3 a.m., trying to get a message that the National Broadcasting Company in San Francisco was relaying to me via Guam. And there would, I knew, be no heat or hot water when I got up.

The once-luxurious Metropole Hotel where I was staying --- like all big buildings in Shanghai in September 1945 --- had been stripped of plumbing parts for scrap iron as more and more of Japan's mainland industries were knocked out by our B-29's. But by the time China's occupiers did this it was already too late.

The Japanese surrendered to the Allies on August 14, 1945. Now, six-and-a-half weeks later, I was about to take off on a special assignment.

Three days earlier, on September 26th, we few correspondents in Shanghai had learned the fate of the captured **"Doolittle flyers"** from Captain Jason Bailey, a U.S. Army investigator for the War Crimes Commission. "There were eight of them," he said "crews of two B-25's under the command of U.S. Army Air Corps General James H. Doolittle that had taken off on April 17, 1942 from the carrier *Hornet* to bomb Tokyo and other cities in Japan. They completed their mission, but, on their return, were forced down for lack of gas and captured by the Japanese in China."

They were flown to Tokyo for 56 days of intense interrogation, then sent to Shanghai and held in the notorious Bridge House until August 28th. [1942] On that day they were taken to Kiangwan Military Prison and brought before a Japanese court-martial that lasted just half an hour. All proceedings were in Japanese. They [the Americans] had no idea of what was going on.

Captain Bailey identified the flyers as George Barr, Jacob de Shazer, William Glover Farrow, Dean Edward Hallmark, Robert L. Hite, Robert J. Meder, Charles J. Neilsen, and Harold A. Spatz. He showed us a translation of the court-martial record. All were sentenced to death. But on October 14, 1942, the Emperor commuted the sentences of five of the men to life imprisonment "under special conditions." The next day, Lieutenant Farrow, Lieutenant Hallmark and Sergeant Spatz were taken to Kiangwan Chinese Cemetery, used by the Japanese as an execution ground, and shot.

The five who were spared were kept in Kiangwan Prison for another six months, then transferred to prisons in Nanking and Peiping. Our recovery teams had got them out (except for one) at war's end in August 1945.

Now, on a golden autumn Saturday in September, we correspondents had been invited by the Army to inspect the cells where the Doolittle flyers had been held. A plane load of correspondents had flown to Peiping earlier in the week, the first such group to enter the old northern capital since Pearl Harbor, four years before.

I left the Metropole and climbed into the jeep with Captain Bailey, Julian Hartt of the International News Service, and an Office of War Information (OWI) photographer, and a Chinese Army Colonel, who was our escort. Passing through Shanghai's outskirts, I saw Chinese farmers busy in the fields, oblivious to the comings and goings of the foreigners all around them, victor and vanquished alike. We went through some gates to a sign reading: "Headquarters Japanese 13th Army, Shanghai Area." This was the building where the Doolittle flyers had been summarily tried and sentenced to death in violation of International Law.

A Japanese officer led us down a narrow corridor leading from the courtroom to the cells --- which were eleven feet high, ten feet deep and four-and-a-half feet wide. Each had a small window eight feet up and a sunken latrine, a one-holer with a wooden cover. A single naked electric bulb hung from the ceiling.

We paused at one. Lt. George Barr occupied this cell," said Captain Bailey, pointing to a message that had been laboriously scratched on a floor board with a thin, sharp object --- a fishbone or a broken button perhaps: *Lt. G. Barr, USAAC - 34th Bomb Sqdn. - Columbia, S.C., USA. Took off from AC hornet 4/17/42 - Bombed Nagoya, Japan - Flew 17 hours to China - No gas. Jumped. Captured 4/18/42*.

Cell number three had been the home of 2nd Lt. Robert J. Meder. We knelt to examine what he had etched on the floor -- a date, his name, rank and serial number then: *U.S. Army Air Corps, B 25 Detach, Plane No. 0398. Two final lines cried out to anyone who might come after him: Notify U.S. Army -- Life Imprisonment.* Apparently, their life sentences "under special conditions" meant solitary confinement. The surviving flyers were so kept thereafter. Robert Meder died in Nanking on December 1, 1943 after suffering from dysentery and beri beri without proper medical attention.

Now a Japanese guide was to take us to the cemetery where the three executions had taken place. We sat down on a wooden bench to wait. A Japanese officer suggested tea. Though neither I nor Hartt had breakfast, we wondered whether we could swallow even a mouthful of tea in the mood of spiritual desolation that had settled over us. Captain Bailey said, indeed, he's like some tea. I believe he enjoyed having the Japs wait on him, and bow to him, more than he wanted tea. We said all right, we'd have some too then.

The guards brought some small tables. Tea cups were set down and a good, green China tea was poured. The Captain, Hartt and myself gulped it down. The Chinese Colonel didn't drink any.

A Japanese non-com arrived carrying a large square box wrapped in unbleached muslin, tied in a knot at the top. The soldier took off his cap, bowed low, then backed away. In a minute he returned with a smaller box wrapped in fine white silk, which he placed atop the larger box and backed off. Another Japanese untied the knot in the wrapping this box, revealing the black stenciled words:
"U S A Commissioned Officer's Ashes." My cup almost fell from my hand. I set it down hard in the saucer and it made a sharp little sound. Julian Hartt's hand doubled into a tight fist as he straightened up. Captain Bailey grew taught and looked up sharply. Captain Maszumi Shimada, the Commandant, arrived, bowing and saluting.

"These are Captain Meder's ashes. They have just arrived from Nanking. You will take them back with you, perhaps?"

It was a sadistic little gesture, timed to perfection, this arrival of the dead flyer's ashes in their urn...amid the tea cups.

"Give the box to me!" Captain Bailey ordered.

Shimada handed him the box. The American officer looked at it silently a moment, resting there on his knees. I put out my hands; he handed me the box without a word. I cradled it in my arms on my lap and bent to hide my face from the inquisitive Japanese around us. Not for worlds would I let them see the tears that I was fighting desperately to hold back

"Open the other box," Captain Bailey ordered.

Captain Shimada spoke to his aide, who untied the knot in the muslin and slid back the cover of the larger box. The stenciling, done by someone unfamiliar with English, read: **U S A Commissioned Officer's Luggages**. Captain Bailey reached in and took out one small object after another.

There was a book of traveler's checks. A personal check book -- the last two stubs for $21.25, the premium on his life insurance policy, and $17 to the U.S.S. *Hornet* mess. There were keepsakes in a mildewed leather case: a photo of a very pretty girl, his Phi Kappa Tau fraternity card, a club membership I.D. Then a compass, a comb and file, a key case, a Social Security card --- And that was about all.

Capt. Bailey replaced the objects, gave orders for the box and the dead flyer's clothes to be placed in the jeep. Then we all stood up. I just naturally clung to the little silk-wrapped box..

We got into the jeep and headed for the cemetery. At the entrance the Chinese Colonel touched my arm and Captain Bailey's. "Would you give me the privilege of sitting here with Lieutenant Meder?" he asked, inclining his head ever so slightly toward the box.

Without a word I handed it to him. Never, I think, have I heard a more gracious sentence, nor one more deeply poignant.

We left the jeep and walked past naked Chinese children huddled around the cemetery gates. They watched us with wide-eyed curiosity. The sun was warm and riding high. We tramped single-file through the high, thick grass, past broken stones and desecrated mounds. Suddenly the guide paused, looked down and spoke to the interpreter, who said, "This is the place."

This was the place, indeed. Here, on October 15, 1942, 2nd Lt. Dean Edward Hallmark, age 27, from Dallas, Texas, pilot; 2nd Lt. William Glover Farrow, age 23, of Darlington, South Carolina, pilot; and Sgt. Harold A. Spatz, 20, machine gunner, were brought from their cells and shot.

"He say that persons who see execution say men had to kneel down. Then guards tie hands to little crosses behind them and Japanese soldiers shoot from the side," explained the interpreter. "They taken in coffins to Japanese crematorium. Ashes go to POW officer. He maybe give to Red Cross."

No receipts for the bodies or ashes were found. The incriminating records of the court-martial and executions were methodically tracked down by the War Crimes Commission, based on information from a civilian employee-witness at the prison.

We turned away from the sad little place, hallowed with American blood. At the gates the Chinese children were eating their rice. They jumped up and with childish glee and waved their chopsticks at us. The Chinese Colonel handed me the little box as I sat down in the jeep. I cradled it in my hands on my lap again, holding it close to me against the bumps and jogs in the uneven road.

We drove back to Shanghai.

END

FAMILY VALUES

in the Context of

CHINESE and AMERICAN CULTURES

by Diana L. Kao, Ph.D.

The family in China, as in elsewhere, is generally considered the basic unit of society. It consists usually of a married couple with children born or adopted, united economically and living together. Some, however, might disagree, and would like to include in a family an unmarried but cohabited, or even a homosexual couple.

The objective of this paper is to explore the differences in family values between China and the united States, as well as between their respective changes through the years.

The family system in China is quite different from that of the United States owing to their respective differences in cultural backgrounds and economic conditions. In a traditional Chinese family, a woman, as a dependent member in the family, had to observe three phases of obedience [to her father before marriage, to her husband after marriage, and to her grown-up son after the death of her husband], and four aspects of virtue [her demeanor, her speech, her employment, and her womanly virtue].

With the establishment of the nationalist Republic of China in 1912, equality of the sexes was advocated, i.e., emancipation of women, discipline of children, and equality of women in property rights, education, and jobs. The emergence of this trend marked the beginning of the disintegration of the traditional Chinese family associated with Confucianism. Under the present Nationalist regime on Taiwan, women have become increasingly active in all spheres of life, even in the political arena. Some of them serve as national delegates in the government.

Meanwhile, interest in family issues has surfaced. Probably under the impact of Western influence, the *Central Daily News* on Taiwan sponsored a conference on March 2, 1993 to deal with the social problems of the Chinese family. The conference was participated by people in various walks of life, including professors, scholars, writers, school administrators, etc. Topics discussed covered parent education, children discipline, preserving Chinese culture in the family, and orientation of the family in a changing environment, among others. Much attention has been directed to reform and strengthening of the family.

Before the Communists took over control of Mainland China in 1949, leftist writers had attacked the traditional Chinese family system, the unequality of the sexes, and arranged marriages of young people by their parents. Since 1949, the Communist regime has made drastic changes in the traditional Chinese family. The communists have brought family changes throughout the state, and enforced the marriage code more seriously than before. Freedom of choice in marriage partners and freedom of divorce are both recognized, though marriage based on romanticism is not encouraged. The emphasis is on loyalty to the state, rather than individual loyalty to the family. In other words, primary emphasis is on ideology and interest of the state. Bigamy and concubinage has been eliminated; marriage age has been increased; birth control, limiting the birth of one child per couple, has been the policy in recent years. This policy has led to female infanticide or abandonment of female infants.

The Communist regime aims to replace the role of the family by taking over the control of every citizen in the country without interference from the family. The functions of the kinship system and of other related institutions have thus been tremendously curtailed.

In the United States, from the end of the 18th to the beginning of the 19th century, men worked at home. following the Industrial Revolution, handicraft tools were replaced with power-driven machines, leading to large concentration of industry in large establishments. A lot of men then worked in the factories. Women took over the role of child nurturing. Later, however, as women joined the labor force, and became economically independent, they began to demand equality of the sexes, and divorce became more common. Now, men have been helping with caring for children, and sharing in household work, so as to ease the stress of women having to work and to do household work as well.

In recent years, the birth rate to single mothers in the United States has increased, leading to a high of 35% of all births in 1991. The reason is that young people whose earnings have been falling are less likely to get married. In addition, more fathers have deserted their wives and children, leading to an increase in single-parent families. The unwed single mother, usually with little or no skill, are at the poverty level, and have to struggle to support themselves and their children on their own. Receiving low welfare air and low pay, or even unemployed, they tend to become alcoholics or drug addicts. As to the delinquents in such families, they are likely to be removed from home by the social system, thus penalizing the poor.

In order to solve these problems, we need to establish a job-training program, so that the little or unskilled parent can earn a decent living. There should also be an adequate day-care center for the children, so that the mother can go out to work. In addition, a low-income family needs affordable housing, health care, and mental-health clinics.

The measures mentioned above need to be continuously maintained. There should be continuous provision of preventive information, comprehensive coverage of multiple needs, and provision of home leave by employers to workers, when necessary.

In recent years, the American family has been on the decline, owing to a number of factors, such as divorce, child abuse, use of drugs, violent movies and crimes, etc. On the whole, Americans, becoming increasingly self-reliant and individualistic, are caring less and less for the commonly recognized family. The term "family" has assumed diverse and devious forms, as follows:

1. A married couple with or without children.
2. An unmarried couple living together.
3. A single unwed mother living with children from different fathers.
4. A single married mother deserted or divorced from her husband.
5. A homosexual couple living together.

A married couple may choose to have or not to have children by various methods. If they prefer to have children, they may, in addition to having a natural child birth by the mother herself, adopt a baby, or have a test-tube baby, contract a surrogate mother to bear the child, or use a sperm from a sperm-storage factory. If the couple prefer not to have children, they may resort to birth control, abortion, having the child adopted by someone else, abandoning the baby, or infanticide. With advanced procreation biology, a grand-mother may be made pregnant by carrying her daughter's fertilized egg transplanted into her womb. Thus one may have a child without sex, and sex without a child.

Furthermore, with Americans placing strong emphasis on the pioneering spirit of individualism, their family is seldom as close-knit as that of the Chinese. In the United States, old parents usually feel guilty to impose on their children for care and financial support. When they are no longer able to take care of themselves, they would most likely be placed in a nursing home.

On the other, a Chinese family in the United States is not entirely free of family problems. In a mixed cultural environment, the older generation of Chinese in New York City, for instance, tend to be rather conservative, and preserving the old Chinese cultural pattern. They have not participated in any change in their own cultural pattern since they left China, nor have they been quite assimilated to the new American cultural pattern owing to language handicap and other factors. On the other hand, their children, who came to the United States at an early age or were born and educated here, would speak mostly English and hardly any Chinese. With differences in language and cultural orientation, the two generations, the old and the young, have difficulty in mutual communication, and often do not see things eye-to-eye. There are also some Chinese who came here as adults and professed to be "old fashioned" in valuing the old Chinese

Cultural pattern. Having stayed here for sometime, however, they would give up their belief in the old Chinese family system, and proclaim to value "privacy" above anything else; their own interest comes first before their obligation to the old folks.

Similarly, the same problem of mutual understanding exists among people of the same generation. Those who came to the united States after adolescence are most likely to retain the Chinese language and cultural pattern. They are referred to as juk-haak, meaning "block-head", who are obstinate and unable to see how things work in a new environment in the United States. The other group of Chinese youths consists of those who are native born or came to the United States at an early age. They are referred to as juk-sing, meaning "empty vessel" or "hollow scoop", and are considered not to understand anything.

Thus, there is difficulty in mutual communication not only between the old and the young, but also among the young themselves. In cases of generation gap, parents should show their younger generation compassion, love, trust, friendship, guidance, and advice. Children should reciprocate on their part with understanding, care, and respect for their elders.

The Chinese Benevolent Association in New York Chinatown has established an after-school-hour Overseas Chinese School to instill in these young Chinese people some knowledge and appreciation of their own native custom and culture. This is to prevent these young overseas Chinese from becoming "bananas", so to speak [i.e., yellow outside and white inside]. This would help the young Chinese people with getting on the main stream in America, while living in harmony with their elders at home.

Furthermore, there should be a network of factors for building a good family. the primary factor consists in home education, with the parents serving as role models for the young. Outside the family, the following units may also offer assistance to the family in one way or another:

1. The school teachers and the PTA.
2. The church ministers.
3. The social workers in setting up programs to help meet the multiple needs of the family.
4. The employers to give their employees home leave, when necessary.
5. Financial assistance by government agencies for the unemployed and the underpaid workers, if necessary, etc.

Meanwhile, researches and investigations should be undertaken to tackle with family problems and the causes for the decline of the family. For the welfare of the individual, the society, and the country, the family is too important an issue to be ignored or sacrificed by any institutions or organizations concerned.

+++++

TAOISM and FEMINISM

by Ellen M. Chen, Ph.D.

The feminist movement in the West has many facets and as an evolving philosophy cannot be pinned down to any one particular position. This paper goes beyond political debate to the metaphysical grounding of a feminism from the Taoist perspective: it vindicates the feminine traits as characteristics of the divine.

A.   The Feminist Revolt in the West.

The woman's liberation movement began as a rebellion not so much against convention as against nature, which by imposing on women the reproductive functions has been their real oppressor. radical feminists rebelled against women's biological roles. To them the real struggle for women is between the individual and the species, between what the woman as an individual wants and what the species dictates to her. Woman has so far served as the vehicle for the perpetuation of the species. While a man is marked by his individuality, hence Aristotle defines substance or primary being as an "individual" and a "this," a woman, like the Aristotelian matter, has no self - identity without a man: she belongs to her father when young, her husband after marriage, and her son in widowhood. Liberty for women means the freedom to put aside their reproductive fertility for pursuits which in the past were prerogatives of men.

This anti - nature stance against women's fate, repudiating women's gender roles, is but the continuation of the historical process of the struggle between humans and nature. Just as the former slaves, aided by machines which serve as the new slaves, now join the ranks of their former masters, women hope to join the ranks of men when they are liberated by science and technology from the burden of child-bearing and child-rearing. feminists believe that equality comes to women only if they become like men. In holding man up as the standard, the feminist movement acknowledges the superiority of man's mode of existence.

To depict woman's struggle as one between the individual and the species is misleading. Species life is not restricted to biology; it is also cultural life. For Hegel, every individual is material for the realization of the universal, what he calls the "cunning of reason." If survival of the species require women to give up their individuality to play the role of the goddess of fertility, it equally required men to give up their individuality to conform to the warrior archetype of power and aggression: the hero's greatness as an individual is measured by how much he contributes to the species life, thus men have been as much subjected to cultural bondage as women to biological bondage.

Since humans are social beings, the war against the species is a false war. All individual accomplishments eventually accrue to the species. The modern valuation on individual rights and freedoms, by allowing the individuals to develop to their full, are still for the enrichment of the species. The issue is not whether the individual serves the interest of the species, but whether the individual should have a choice in the mode serving the species. Contemporary liberation movements correctly argue that when liberty and equality extend to all individuals regardless of sex, color or creed, the species is better served. As early as the nineteenth century, J.S. Mill in *The Subjection of Women* already pointed out the need to look at women as individuals, not as confined in her gender role.

If there was a historical necessity for the existence of slavery, the same historical necessity existed for the "oppression" of women. Women were restricted to the roles of child-bearing and child-rearing in the past when the survival of the species was a priority. Women's historical mission has been so successfully accomplished today the human species is literally crowding out other species on the planet earth. The unrestricted propagation of human life on earth is causing not only the extinction of other life forms, it may be ultimately detrimental to human survival. Patriarchal societies, granting freedom and individuality to dominant males, may have contributed to the prosperity of the human species in the past. Today, it is obvious that societies in which women are free from natural and culturally imposed fetters to develop to their fullest potentials are more dynamic and creative societies.

Unlike men who cannot bear children thus are confined to contribute to the species life in the cultural sphere, women can be fertile both culturally and biologically. Aristotle compares the mind to an empty receptacle which is nothing before it thinks. In the same way he compares the female womb to a receptacle for the growth of the fetus, itself contributing nothing to the form of the fetus, itself contributing nothing to the form of the fetus. His erroneous biology aside, it is clear that women , unlike men, have two receptacles or wombs, one intellectual and another biological. This means that today women should be able to exercise a genuine career choice, to develop either one or both or none of these receptacles. Hence the question asked by Professor Higgins in *My Fair Lady:* "Why can't a woman be like a man?" is answered with a resounding "Oh, yes, she can!" though since she has two wombs, a woman is always **more than a man.**

Instead of asking whether a woman ought to be like a man, we may ask whether a man ought to be like a woman. I agree with Eric Erickson that men's way of doing things has led us to a number of dead ends, thus for women to imitate men's way would be no solution for them or for the human race.

B. Taoist Theory of the Feminine

In the *Genesis* death was due to sin first committed by a woman; in Taoism the divine is feminine and one who confers immortality is the Queen Mother of the West. Perishing is a built-in feature of *yang*, the masculine, but *yin,* the feminine, is ever abiding. While the Confucian sage dwells in *yang*, Taoist men have always wanted to be like women. The *Huai-nan Tzu* says: "The exemplary man dwells in *yin,* the crowd dwells in *yang:* "Therefore the sage abides by the light of Tao, he embraces the female way" [17/111]. The *Classic of Su Nu* says: **"Women is superior to man in the same way that water is superior to fire."**

In Greek mythology [Hesiod, *Theogony* 116] the Chaos womb eventually becomes in Aristotle ;matter, a pure potentiality without actuality, and a principle banished from the divine. Taoism supplies a feminine paradigm for the theory of the divine. The Taoist *wu* as nothing or emptiness is the deification of the with what Max Kaltenmark calls "the theme of the mother" and the "Primacy of the Feminine." [*Lao Tzu and Taoism,* Stanford University Press, 1969, pg. 37 & 58]. I shall not elaborate this point here, but shall merely quote a passage from an article I wrote years ago:

> All the symbols of the Great Mother -- dark, night, chasm, cave, abyss, valley, depths, womb -- are present in the descriptions of Tao. Tao is the empty vessel (ch. 4), the bellows (ch. 5), the dark (ch.1), unborn preceding all gods (ch.4), the mystical female which is the door of heaven and earth (ch6), the mother (chs. 1,20.25,52), the hen (chs. 10, 28), the mare (chs 6, 61), the Great Mother (chs 25, 34). Tao is also water (chs. 8, 78) that nourishes and benefits all things, the valley (chs. 6, 28, 32, 39, 41) that is productive due to its lowliness. Tao as *wu* is the archetypal *en sich,* the Urobores, the Archetypal Feminine, which contains and produces all things from within its emptiness (chs. 40, 42) [*History of Religions, 14/1:53*].

The *Tao Te Ching* holds the feminine characteristics of tenderness, caring self-donation and passivity, essential for the nurturing of life, to be divine attributes; it calls the masculine way, that of the strong, unbending and aggressive, ways to early death (chs. 42, 55, 76). Taoism harps on the bliss of the unconscious, instinctual life. It emphasizes not individuality, independence and self-sufficiency, as enumerated by Aristotle and upheld in Western metaphysic, but the harmony and rooted-ness of all beings in the matrix. According to the *Tao Te Ching*, only what has no self-identity is long lasting: "Heaven and earth are long lasting. Why are heaven and earth long-lasting? Because they do not live for self" (ch. 7). As the everlasting Tao is nameless, the Taoist sage is also nameless.

Taoism does not tell woman to imitate man, it tells man to return to woman. This the eternal relationship between the feminine and the masculine. The males [*yang*], representing ego and individuality, are transient actors on the "stage of life." They pertain to perishing [See Shao Yung, *The Supreme Principle Governing the World*]. By their existence and accomplishments the world is what it is, a world not only of nature, but of culture and adventure.

It is the man's fate to accomplish and perish; it is woman's role to play the persistent ground against which changes can become manifest. As the carrier of life, woman rather than man represents immortal life: she is the primordial mother, his companion in life, receiving and fructifying his seed, thus conferring on him a semblance of immortality after he has played out his role and departed. The most tragic yet most joyful moment of a woman's life is to discover that she is pregnant with the child of her dead lover. In this way woman imitates the earth, which sprouts forth with new life every spring after the devastations of winter; what has perished has returned in a new form. This is the eternal return of life to earth, no matter how fleeting and painful individual life is. The woman is thus Plato's receptacle, Aristotle's matter, the soil where the seeds of life are sown and germinate, as well as the tragic heroine and the sorrowful mother [the Pieta] who receives back her dead children. The woman is all these exactly because she has no self - identity: *yang* comes and goes, but *yin* abides to serve as the substratum and continuum.

As individuals with individual identies all beings, male or female, are subject to perishing. Even the divine, as the individual being or *yang*, perishes, hence the travail of deity [*ti*] in the *Shuo Kua, The book of Changes*. In Taoism feminism means that women and men are both free to play the role of the masculine or feminine. The woman is free to opt for the role of *yang*, to become an achieving, hence perishing individual; the man, like the Taoist sage, may prefer to reside in the *yin*, identifying with the ever transforming everlasting Tao.

+++++

ANCIENT WISDOM INSPIRES
NEW APPROACH TO
SINGING and SPEAKING

by Stephen Chun-Tao Chen

Inspired by ancient wisdom of harmony, I have created a new approach to transforming the singing and speaking voice   **The TAO of VOICE.**   My approach is a successful integration of ancient Chinese philosophy and breathing practices [*ch'i*] with the best of Western vocal techniques as well as important psycho-physical discoveries of my own.

This revolutionary approach which has received very encouraging support and press comments, aims at bringing voice, body, mind and spirit into harmony. It can dramatically free and enrich your voice, improve vocal quality, power, range, dynamics and flexibility, and enhance expressive communication and performance.

It is a great joyful feeling to experience the transformation of one's voice, a one-of-a-kind instrument that expresses one's thoughts and emotions more directly than any other. In my book and classes and workshops, I want to share my approach with those people who are seeking new ways to realize the full potential of their voice.

The elusive balance of contradiction in the standard Western approach to vocal technique---tightening the diaphragm without producing tension, "projecting" the voice without strain---takes years to achieve. Many singers and speakers have damaged their voice in pursuit of this goal. Many years meant a lot of frustration, a lot of money and a lot of tension which was reflected in the voice.

My students at New York University in the early seventies implored me : "Isn't there any Chinese wisdom you can add to make this process faster and less frustrating?" As it happens I had already been exploring certain concepts behind the Chinese health exercises that had been a part of my upbringing. I was encouraged to continue my explorations of *T'ai Chi* movement and breathing [*ch'i*], as well as the ancient Taoist philosophy behind them.

Taoism, a Chinese philosophy, the roots of which have been traced back to 3,000 BC., is the basis of every aspect of Chinese intellectual and artistic life---even medicine.

The foundation of Taoism is the harmonious interplay of opposing forces---*Yin* and *Yang*---in a continuous flow of energy. Darkness and light, softness and firmness, female and male, back and forth, loud and soft, high and low, fast and slow.... one cannot exist without the other and each flowing into the opposite containing rather than excluding it. The resulting continuous circular movement is the basis for everything in the Universe.

"Tao is cyclical in its movement," stated Lao Tzu, founder of Taoism, in describing the importance of continuous circular movement and the harmonious interplay of opposite forces.

The wonder of curricular movement is all around us---from the turning of wheels, to the motion of walking feet, to the spinning of the earth on its axis. In his book *"The Tao of Physics,"*, the American physicist Fritjof Capra confirmed the important scientific aspects of Taoism including the circular movement and the interplay of opposite forces.

The best singers are those who can create a balanced energy flow for the voice. Circular movement and harmonious inter play of opposite forces can help a person to gain balanced energy flow in a reasonably short period of time. This is one of the most important discoveries in my method.

To use my method to improve the speaking voice [including quality and richness] can achieve good results quite quickly. My method can benefit beginners as well as professionals who have an open mind and are willing to set aside old habits.

The regenerative powers of my method and the joy produced by harmonious coordination of mind, body, spirit and voice can be transmitted to others. And its effects are not limited to singing. It has a wonderful effect of helping people to supplement or complete what they are in need of. As Dr. Jean Houston says in introduction to my book: *The Tao of Voice*: "Singing becomes a joy, an art and a mystery---a gift of healing the self and others...One grows as one sings the awakening of one's being."

Singing thus becomes, not only an end in itself, but a means of achieving a better balance in one's life and a way of bringing people together. I dedicate my book to "people who use their voices to promote peace and harmony around the world.

+++++

Chapter IX

APPENDICES

Congratulatory Message
to the 27th General Conference
of the
World League for Freedom and Democracy

by

Lee Teng-hui, Ph.D.

President
Republic of China

July 28, 1995

President Chao and Delegates to the 27th General Conference of the World League for Freedom and Democracy :

It is highly significant that the World League for Freedom and Democracy convenes its 27th General Conference in New York City as the World celebrates the 50th anniversary of the signing of the United nations Charger. The theme of this conference --- "Global Cooperation for Better Standards of Life for All" ---matches accidentally with the objectives of peace, equality, justice, and development proclaimed in the UN Charter. On behalf of the government and people of the republic of China, I would like to extend to you my warmest greetings.

With the end of the Cold War, the world is moving toward conciliation and cooperation. The pursuit of democracy, economic liberalization, human rights, and equality has become deeply rooted in the people's consciousness, constituting a driving force for building a new world order and heralding a bright future for our world.

However, if we take a close look at the current world situation, we can see many complex variables lurking beneath the surface. Frequent regional conflicts and endless economic and environmental problem urgently await solutions through the joint efforts of intelligent people. As a member of the World League for Freedom and Democracy and the international community, the Republic of China on Taiwan is willing to pay back the global community with the experience it has gained from political economic, and cultural achievements and to shoulder its international responsibilities for the benefit of world peace and prosperity.

On this festive occasion, I sincerely hope that all members of the League will maintain its tradition of perseverance and struggle, be sensible of the developments in the world situation, and unite the worldwide forces of justice to support **ROC** participation in the United Nations and other world organizations. I also hope you will continue to promote the global movement for freedom and democracy, and create a new era of world peace, cooperation, and prosperity.

Finally, I wish this conference great success and each one of you good health and happiness.

OPENING ADDRESS OF THE 27TH ANNUAL CONFERENCE OF THE WORLD LEAGUE FOR FREEDOM AND DEMOCRACY

by Tze-Chi Chao, LL.D. and WLFD President

Today, the 27th World League for Freedom and Democracy General Conference convenes in grand fashion in the city of New York in the United States of America, an event which coincides with the 50th anniversary of the founding of the United Nations. In addition to expressing our heartfelt remembrances here on this joyous occasion, we also raise high the banner of "Global Cooperation for Better Standards of Life for All" in carrying out the fundamental spirit of the United Nations Charter as our League embarks upon a new struggle.

The second World War was concluded 50 years ago, yet over the past half-century the fact that people in many parts of the world remain subject to the chaos of war, poverty and famine instills in us a keen sense of sorrow and regret. Until only a few years ago, the firm alliance of the forces of justice was engaged in a tireless effort to disperse little-by-little the dark clouds hanging over the world situation, as the enslaving communist regimes collapsed in disorder and the forces of freedom and democracy were in universal ascendance.

In promoting this epochal period of transition, the World League for Freedom and Democracy, with the heart and strength of each and every member united as one, put forth an active contribution. To the remnant communist regimes, we have applied a tremendous spiritual pressure; to the European nations of the bygone totalitarian bloc, we have opened roads to the future; to the developing nations around the globe, we have imported the collective consciousness of cooperative economic development; to all peoples of the world, we have championed the concepts of freedom, democracy and human rights. Confronting every source of chaos and unrest in every locale, we have sought through reason and fraternity to extricate disputes or disruptions and guide humanity toward an auspicious peace. In particular, as the United Nations body requires assistance from non-governmental organizations in order to safeguard world peace, the World League has accordingly persevered in its efforts, in ever-greater coordination with the U.S., to shoulder the duties of this new era.

On the basis of the above-described accumulation of experience, and with the results of research by numerous scholars and experts, we have reaped a profound understanding, with strengthened convictions and courage, at the at advent of the 21st century, that we must strive for an even greater prosperity for all humanity.

We firmly believe that only by maintaining a durable world peace can a stable foundation be established for human prosperity. Thus, we appeal to all nations of the world, its peoples, religions, political organizations and interest groups, to renounce extremist opposition or confrontation, and furthermore, to avoid such precipitates to war and violence, using our compassion to maintain mutual interest and safety, and through this cooperation, to abandon the mistaken concept of resolving problems by means of force or violence.

We firmly believe that the totalitarian nations which still exist today, although strengthened by economic developments, constitute the primary source of instability in the modern world as they continue to regress the growth of freedom and democracy. We hope they will abandon their plans for weapons proliferation, cease their schemes to foment war and unrest through manipulation of ethnic nationalism, and allow their citizens to fully enjoy freedom, democracy and human rights. Only then can order return to the world situation and a true peace be achieved.

We firmly believe that mutually beneficial economic cooperation and flow of trade is the basic means for advancement of human prosperity. Excessive protectionism and severe retaliation are contradictory to the spirit of economic cooperation and can easily create a global economic and trade crisis. We urge that the developed countries of the world must bring into full play the morality and courage exemplified by great nations, and assist people in backward areas in eliminating the pain of poverty, natural disaster, famine, disease and hunger, so that the lives of all peoples of the world may attain reasonable safeguards and equitable development.

The establishment of the United Nations fifty years ago represents the most significant memorial day in history. At that time, the surrender of the Axis Powers brought an end to the protracted conflict of the Second World War. Today, although the U.N. organizational structure continues to expand, its membership is more complex, and, despite a successive collapse of the communist regimes, numerous forms of ideological war and conflict continue to occur in international society. Thus, United Nations Secretary-General Boutros Boutros-Ghali stated at the 47th Conference of U.N. Nongovernmental Organizations that maintenance of a comprehensive and meaningful peace cannot be accomplished by the U.N. system, or by governments, alone. Rather, nongovernmental organizations, academic institutions, parliaments, business and professional organizations, mass media and the publishing industry must all be involved in the sacred mission of peace-keeping.

The World League, under this prudent call to action, supports Secretary-General Boutros-Ghali's view, not only becoming a member of the U.S. Nongovernmental Organizations, but moreover, through full assistance to the United Nations from an unprejudiced standpoint, active contribution of resources, advancement of peace and democratization in international society, and through mediation of international disputes and issues concerning human rights or humanitarian protection. But, the World League also wishes to suggest to the leadership of the United Nations Organization that in carrying out the basic spirit of universality among U.N. member-countries, the doors of this international body must be opened to all sovereign nations which truly uphold the principles of the U.N. Charter. Only then can a long-lasting prosperity for all nations and peoples truly be created.

Loyal and faithful friends of the World League for Freedom and Democracy, the present times require our full strength and continued promotion of freedom, democracy, prosperity and equitable well-being for all peoples of the world. Let us then come together and redouble our efforts in fulfillment of this epochal mission.

+++++

REPORT OF THE WLFD SECRETARIAT
TO ITS 27TH ANNUAL CONFERENCE

by Jai-Seung Woo, Ph.D.
Secretary-General W.L.F.D.

We all recall that the WLFD has witnessed a very important and great achievement in its history by the significant choice of the city of Moscow as the venue for the last 1994 WLFD General Conference under the able and outstanding leadership of Hon. Dr. Gavriil Popov, and Dr. Nicholas Lutsenko. And with one strong accord, we express our deepest appreciation even as of now to them for their invaluable leadership and services on that occasion.

Changes in the global situation as we enter the 21st century have been quite dramatic. All these momentous developments in the international arena are speedily taking place at this crucial stage of the new world order for peace, political and economic advancement, and the global cooperation in the areas of institutionalizing social development, environmental protection, lasting human rights ideals for all mankind.

These heart-warming changes are indeed inspirational as we celebrate the 50th year milestone of the founding of the United Nations, whose hopes and aspirations the WLFD has shared for past forty-years.

I am particularly happy to draw your attention and that of all present at this occasion that the situation in the Korean Peninsula has witnessed a considerable degree of positive change, and it is my fervent hope that more such events will be in succession in the coming years.

An agreement has been reached between the United States and North Korea in their talks on the nuclear issue. North Korea is to receive South Korean-made light water nuclear reactors to serve her needs in nuclear energy. Fuel supply arrangements have been made for shipments to North Korea to meet the power supply needs in the country.

The Government of the Republic of Korea has also begun shipment of 150,000 tons of rice, free of charge to North Korea as a gesture to help avert imminent food shortages and the attendant hardships on the people.

Japan has also agreed for her assistance in a similar direction to supply rice to North Korea in a low interest rate and long-term repayment agreement.

The sincere commitment to these encouraging agreements by the North Korean authorities, however, remains to be confirmed when one considers past experiences.

Evidently however, these good developments can not be the same for the situation in the entire Asia. While it is most heart warming and quite refreshing to witness progressive developments in many areas, other areas in the region continue to be saddled with all manner of economic and political instability and insecurity.

As highlighted in his vivid explanatory account of events in Asia, Dr. Samuel P. Huntington [Professor, Harvard University] mentioned in an address delivered recently in Seoul that the specific seeds of conflicts in Asia are very alarming, and they are as listed:

1) The divided countries: Korea and China
2) Unresolved territorial issues: the northern islands of Japan,
    Chinese boundaries with India and Russia,
    competing claims to the South China Sea.
3) Insurgencies of secessionist movements in Mindanao, East Timor, Tibet,
    southern Thailand, and eastern Burma.
4) Arms build-ups in which all east Asian nations are contributing and:
5) Nuclear weapons, acquisition of which is an active goal of North Korea and a
    potential goal of Japan.

These to my mind, are really dangerous, and they call for urgent and concerted International approach for peaceful solutions.

As if these very disturbing International conflicts are not enough for the global community, genocide, mass killings and various human rights abuses continue to be the order of events in war-torn former Yugoslavia, Rwanda, Liberia, Algeria and else where. These conflicts if not given prompt and appropriate attention could easily spread to many other areas, as there are countries sitting so calmly on various "political and economic time-bombs" whose future explosions could be disastrous for all of us.

In view of the changing times with new challenges, hopes and aspirations for all mankind, I would like to urge all present here at this Conference and the entire International community to work effectively towards the establishment of new innovations, mechanisms and structures needed to ensure peace, freedom and prosperity for our entire human race.

+++++

EPILOGUE

Edited by publisher Robert E. Whittaker

Dr. Victor T. H. Tsuan wrote these important words of wisdom in the book titled: *Sixty Years of Shanghai "Tiffin" Perspective.* The publisher has been granted permission to include them here again.

"When I was being sworn in to become a naturalized American citizen some years ago, the federal judge read a brief statement which included this sentence; *"As a rule naturalized American citizens are more patriotic than native born Americans."*

"Indeed, I too find this to be true. The reason is that the overwhelming majority of native-born Americans take for granted the American way of life. On the other hand, since most of us naturalized American citizens came from the captive nations and have experienced so much suffering before entering this great country, we naturally appreciate deeply, the freedom and the opportunities that America affords us under its' democratic system."

Likewise, these same sentiments can be echoed by those "Old China Hands" born overseas and who lived for years in the Orient. (editor)

"Every patriotic American today wonders at what has happened to America, with our difficulty in coping with serious problems such as crime, disorder, terrorism, unemployment, inflation and government deficits."

"Do you realize that in the United States today it is not political oppression that threatens us, but the decline of our confidence in American government and the diminishing of human freedom due to Communist (*Socialist*) [editor], subversive activities. Unfortunately the great majority of American people, who have had no personal experience, would disbelieve such facts."

"**The Communist Rules for Revolution** was given to me by Rosalie Smith Davenport, who was the second Vice President of the Shanghai *Tiffin* Club while I was President. She had obtained it from an ex KGB agent."

(1) Corrupt the young; get them away from religion. Get them interested in sex. Make them superficial; destroy their ruggedness.
(2) Plant the seeds of Communism \ Socialism in schools and universities.
(3) Get control of all means of publicity and the media. Thereby:
*   A. Get people's mind off their government by focusing their attention on athletics, sexy books, plays, video and other trivialities.*

B. *Divide the people into hostile groups by constantly harping on controversial matters of no importance.*

C. *Destroy the people's faith in their natural leaders by holding the latter up to contempt, ridicule and disgrace.*

D. *Always preach true democracy, but seize power as fast and as ruthlessly as possible.*

E. *By encouraging government extravagance, destroy its credit, produce fear of inflation with rising prices and general discontent.*

F. *Incite unnecessary strikes in vital industries, encourage civil disorders and foster a soft and lenient attitude on part of government and law enforcement to such lawlessness.*

G. *By specious argument, cause the breakdown of the old moral virtues -- honesty, sobriety, self-restraint, faith in the pledged word and ambition.*

(4) *Cause the registration of all fire-arms on some pretext, with the intent of confiscating them and leaving the populace helpless.*

"As the Communist world falls further behind economically, the non-communist world is moving into a new technological age. The contrast is so great, we firmly believe that the communist parties all over the world can no longer resist man's powerful desire for freedom, for a better standard of living and for self-determination. World communism has already passed its' zenith and will rapidly decline; the final bankruptcy of the communist system is only a question of time."

Victor T. H. Tsuan, Ph.D.

The publisher would add to the "Communist \ Socialist Blueprint for Revolution" as it pertains to the United States: [not in order of importance]

* Encourage vast numbers of the American populace to become dependent on welfare programs.
* Reward single parent households.
* Subsidize "babies" having babies.
* "Dumb down" education.
* Promote affirmative-action racism.
* Reward mediocrity, but not excellence.
* Sanction homosexuality.
* Foster class envy.
* Corrupt the government and its leaders
* Degrade the judicial \ legal system.
* Foment racial and religious bigotry.
* Foster intolerance towards <u>legal</u> immigrants.
* Promote trade barriers and isolationism

+++++

EPILOGUE II

The Free China Journal published this commentary on March 22, 1996 written by their senior copy editor, <u>Michael Joseph</u>. This was the day before the Republic of China's first presidential elections in China's 5000 year history. It is abridged and printed here by permission.

If the people of Taiwan must have an emotional response to their presidential election, the leaders in Peking seemed to say, then those emotions will be motivated by the mainland and they will not be pleasant. It was the decision-makers in Peking trying to appropriate for their own use the success of democracy on Taiwan.

Those decision-makers of course have a fistful of motivations to try to co-opt the Republic of China's success. They fear they'll lose power after the demise of aged patriarch Deng Xiaoping. A thriving democracy just across the Straits would not make the legitimacy of their regime seem quite so questionable if the world could be made to understand that Peking's leaders hold the deed to that island democracy.

But the rest of the world is not so gullible. And the leaders in Peking, though looking ahead to the geopolitical business of the next century, still perceive the rest of the world through lenses made in the first half of the present century.

In the end, Peking's behavior in the last two weeks may be one of the best defenses of democracy in the long-standing argument over whether a Western-style representative government or authoritarianism is the better political system for Asia: If democracy on an island of 21 million people can cause such impulsive and irrational behavior among the leaders of a population of 1.2 billion, then that democracy must be a potent force indeed, an evil threat to be scared off by extremely high-profile fireworks.

All of China, to be sure, will the world's next super-power. China is the anchor of Asia and Asia's time has come. But that does not mean that the next century must belong only to the 500 or so Chinese Communist Party elites. Those elites are now monopolizing state power on the mainland and calling all the shots, including the missile shots aimed to steal an election that the people of Taiwan have worked hard for decades to make their own.

Yes, the 21st Century may well belong to China but tomorrow, March 23, 1996 belongs to Taiwan.

EPILOGUE III

This is an abridged version of a speech delivered Nov. 9, 1995, by **Fredrick F. Chien**, *Ph.D. ROC Minister of Foreign Affairs, at Arizona State University in Tempe, Arizona. The speech, titled* "*Implementation of the Taiwan Relations Act: Assessment and Expectations,*" *was the keynote address at a conference on the Taiwan Relations Act.*
It was published in the Free China Journal on December 1, 1995. It is printed here by permission.

Strong Relations

In almost every way, other than diplomatic recognition, the Taiwan Relations Act has enabled four American administrations to continue strong and friendly ties with the ROC and the Chinese people on Taiwan.

As specific examples of these bonds, let me acknowledge the U.S. government's close cooperation with us on environmental, telecommunications, automated machinery, computers, and petrochemical matters. In fact, we are increasing our investments daily in U.S. petrochemical and high-tech industries, a trend that offers financial support to American companies seeking new partners.

Related to this development, last September (1995) we signed the ROC-U.S. trade and investment Framework Agreement. In March of this year (1995) we held the first bilateral consultation meetings in Washington, D.C. This new structure was built in order to make our economic cooperation with the United States closer than ever.

Moreover, the ROC is right now promoting an Asia-Pacific regional operations center plan. It is based upon our central geographic location, our well-trained and productive work force and our strong economic ties with almost every country in the region. We especial welcome participation in the plan by the U.S. multinational corporations and believe that by establishing a strategic operations alliance with ROC firms, U.S. enterprises will be able to expand their own markets throughout the region.

These projects exist thanks to the constant force of the Taiwan Relations Act. There is, however, a major impediment that threatens to disrupt the spirit of the law. I am referring to the persistent, unyielding interference of the Chinese Communists.

They see our national power steadily growing. They see that the building of our democratic institutions is nearly completed. They see our efforts increasing to secure for our people the right of equal representation in the international community.

In reaction, the mainland government tries to squeeze and suppress our international space. They seek to block our participation in world and regional financial, health, welfare, economic, technological and environmental activities and organizations of all kinds.

This harsh behavior is seriously affecting the ROC's opportunities for continued progress and development. It impacts cruelly on our people's basic human rights and welfare. Surely, the 21 million free people in Taiwan are fully entitled and qualified to active representation in all world organizations and operations.

U.S. Assurances

Fortunately, the implementation of the Taiwan Relations act demonstrates that the U.S. government does not accept this unfair treatment by communist China or the motive in back of it. The American government has never recognized Peking's claim of sovereignty over Taiwan. Washington has consistently held that the U.S. has not altered its position regarding sovereignty and that the issue "is a matter for the Chinese parties to decide themselves." This was one of the six assurances that President Reagan gave to the ROC before issuing the 1982 U.S. - Mainland Joint Communique.

In closing, it is my sincere hope and expectation that the U.S. government will continue to maintain the full spirit of the Taiwan Relations Act so as:

---To help us resist external military and other threats;

 ---To support our participation in international organizations in order to uphold the wishes of our people and their basic human rights;

---To make the "one China" policy clear, with its concept of two equal political entities;

---And to reject communist China's sovereignty claim.

Finally, I also expect that our friends in the U.S. Congress will continue in their strong oversight role, which has been a pillar of maintaining our long friendship with the United States and American support of our cause.

+++++

IN THE ROC GLOBAL VICTORY FOR DEMOCRACY

*This is an abridged adaptation of an address by **ROC Government Information Office, Director-General Jason C. Hu, Ph.D.** on March 26, 1996 to the American Enterprise Institute in Washington, D.C. It was published in **The Free China Journal** on April 26, 1996 and is printed here by permission.*

A Chinese First

In the election, the people of Taiwan did just what their government had reassured Peking they were going to do, namely, directly elect for the first time in Chinese history the highest leader of the land, the president of the **Republic of China.** We believe the result was in no way harmful to the people of the Chinese mainland.

The people of Taiwan overwhelmingly elected a leader committed to a One-China policy who has demonstrated the vision to bring their nation through a series of peaceful and positive revolutions, achieving in a few short years since the lifting of martial law what most experts would have estimated to need decades; that is, peaceful multiparty politics and the direct popular election of all top national and provincial leaders.

Consequently, this election has demonstrated that Peking need not fear democracy on Taiwan. By voting for Lee, the people of Taiwan have shown that they want stability and development both at home and in the region. Lee made the position of his government on this issue very clear during his Olin Lecture at Cornell University last June [1995].

"I have repeatedly called on the mainland authorities to end ideological confrontation and to open up a new era of peaceful competition across the Taiwan Straits and reunification. Only by following a 'win-win' strategy will the best interests of all the Chinese people be served. We believe that mutual respect will gradually lead to the peaceful reunification of China under a system of democracy, freedom and equitable distribution of wealth."

People must not ignore the fact that we are one of the largest investors in the mainland and can continue to be a massive source of investment capital, technology transfer and management expertise for them. We want to get along peacefully with our neighbors, and to see the entire Chinese nation ultimately prosper and enjoy the same freedom and democracy that we enjoy today.

If there is any element of cross-Straits competition to be seen here, it is a positive one in which both sides gain. We, the people of Taiwan, have demonstrated to the world, the Chinese mainland and ourselves that Chinese people can develop and nurture democracy---and are determined to play a positive role in assuring regional stability and continued economic growth. There is no harm in that.

If nothing else, the contrast of tension in the Straits in the last weeks before the election with the orderliness and calm of the elections held in the Republic of China helped dramatize for the world what we have been saying all along; Taiwan has achieved democracy with no domestic blood-shed or major turmoil and threatens no one by doing so.

We deserve the affirmation of our fellow members of the international community, not because we wish to take anything away from anyone, but because achieving democracy and being a responsible member of the global village are the responsibilities of all good governments that wish to assure the greatest welfare for their own people and contribute to world peace and prosperity.

As we see now, between the mainland and Taiwan there are perhaps four existing major issues that need to be solved. **One** is a peace agreement between the two sides. **Second** is a high-level meeting, or a summit meeting if possible. **Third**, as the mainland has long desired, the so-called three links: commercial, postal-telecommunications and transportation. **Fourth** is the resumption of talks between the Straits Exchange Foundation and the mainland's Association for Relations Across the Taiwan Straits.

Premier Lien Chan has said already that, if there is no threat, we are ready to discuss with the mainland the possibility of a peace agreement. But we will not do this under threat. On the problem of the so-called three links, we are already saying that the most important transportation links are flights between Taiwan and the mainland. Now in operation are flights which leave Taipei and arrive in Macau, where the aircraft just change their flight numbers and move on to whatever destination they desire on the mainland. Direct or indirect, whatever you want to call it.

We are also proposing the establishment of what we call the offshore transshipment center in Taiwan. foreign vessels calling on Taiwan ports would be able to go directly to ports on the mainland. And talks are under way in Taipei for transportation links under two principles: cargo before passengers, and sea before air. All of these are being discussed.

We have said time and again that we uphold the one-China principle and that we desire peace in the Taiwan Straits. We believe that the ball is now in Peking's court. We hope that leaders on both sides of the Taiwan Straits can think seriously about these things and try to promote a better atmosphere so that we can deal with all these issues in peace and stability.

Finally, in sum, now that the people of Taiwan have spoken their will through the polls and have elected a president who listens to them and knows what is in their hearts, Peking should have no lingering doubts about our commitment to one china, and also our commitment to a democratic, free, prosperous and unified China. The presidential election from the start was an act of democracy, not separatism or independence.

The message conveyed by this election from the people of Taiwan to their leaders, to Peking and the world is that they want dignity, democracy and development for their future.

+++++

FINAL THOUGHTS by the publisher

Chang King-yuh, chairman of the Mainland Affairs Council which deals with relations to Peking is quoted on March 23, 1996 as saying;

"For the first time, Chinese people have elected their President." (The first time in over five thousand years of China's history. Editor's note.)

Chang continues: *"If this is feasible in Taiwan, why not in other areas, like Hong Kong or Macau?"*

These are alarming words to Peking which fears democracy as a threat to Communist Party power. It has been said; "When you fail to learn from history, you are doomed to repeat it."

In 1911 the Manchu court of the Ch'ing Dynasty in Peking was controlled by hundreds of bureaucratic eunuchs and militarists who disregarded the aspirations of the Chinese majority. Imperial Peking was described by one historian as "a termite-riddled floor covered by gold-threaded silk carpets."

When the spark of nationalistic fervor was ignited by the leadership of Sun Yat-sen, the corrupt dynasty crumbled into the dusty basement of history. Today, some 82 years later, the small minority of Communist "ruling eunuchs" on Mainland China are shuffling, once again, on the shaky floor of history.

History will repeat itself! Freedom and Democracy will prevail!

*****

Cites Tao Master's Example

Scholar Says Muck To Settle

By Lao Wei
Special To *FCJ*

As an American born and raised in China, it occurs to me that perhaps the many Chinese intellectuals who have been teaching in various universities within the mainland for the past 40 years have influenced the student activists of the recent pro-democracy movement in the Chinese mainland.

The thought was stimulated by a memory that has remained in my mind for 40 years: During the Chinese Communist conquest of the mainland in 1949, a young Chinese woman I knew was debating with herself whether to flee to the Republic of China in Taiwan or remain in her homeland. This is what she told me as I was leaving China just before the Chinese Communist "People's Army" took over:

"A venerable Master of the Tao recently taught me a profound political lesson. He displayed a crystal bowl filled with clear water. Resting on the bottom was a small amount of red earth.

"He said that if I believed mankind is equal, I should observe a demonstration he was about to perform—and the old sage vigorously stirred the liquid into a red slurry.

"After a short duration, I saw the clear water rise and the mud settle again to the bottom."

As my friend bade me good-bye, she concluded, "I shall remain in my country and help my people during the 'stirring-up-time,' for I know what will eventually happen."

During Mao Tse-tung's so-called "cultural revolution," when hundreds of thousands of students were used by the Chinese Communist leaders to keep "stirring up the red mud" to hide the true conditions in the mainland, these rampaging students lost out on years of education. Many of these illiterates were conscripted into the army and, very possibly, could be the same soldiers who massacred men, women and children in Peking on the weekend of June 3rd and 4th. There are several possible reasons for this horror. The following could be one:

It has been written that on the Chinese social level, the intellectual, which includes the writer, poet and scholar, is ranked the highest. Next comes the fisherman and farmer, for they too create, albeit food. Then comes the artisan and craftsman who carve, paint, sculpt and create with their hands, followed by businessmen and shopkeepers. While the latter group makes more money, the Chinese consider that they make it, more often than not, by devious, manipulative and exploitive methods. Beggars, idlers and thieves are regarded so low as not to be even listed on the social scale. Soldiers are also in this category. An old Chinese adage says: "Nails are not made with good iron... nor soldiers made with good men."

Perhaps today, there is a Chinese poet-general who is able and willing to correctly lead and direct the course of history. Mao said: "Power grows out of the barrel of a gun." So, unfortunately, will this same power be needed to quell the autocratic government officials and bloodthirsty soldiers with their "bottom of the social scale" feeling of inferiority?

Freedom-loving Americans and all people of this planet should observe and be aware of what can transpire when government is usurped by corrupt despots and unmoral opportunists conniving for money and power, at the same time disregarding the wishes of the people.

My tears are as salty as yours, my Chinese friends, but I know you will all finally struggle out of the red mire and into the clear water of freedom and democratic self-fulfillment. I wish you health, happiness and long life.

— Lao Wei (Robert E. Whittaker) was born in Shanghai, China, and educated in the Far East and the United States. He was interned by the Japanese after Pearl Harbor, but released in 1942 as an exchange prisoner and repatriated to the U.S. As a retired Naval Reserve Officer, Master Mariner, film-maker, and poet-writer-scholar, Lao Wei has visited more than 85 countries in Africa, Europe, the Near and Far East, and Central and South America. He presently resides in Wisconsin, U.S.A.

History repeats itself. Peking today, (1996) is again
"stirring up the red muck of Communism"
to obscure their failing policies!   (R.E.W.)

ABOUT THE AUTHORS

AULICK, June L., *Free-lance writer based in New York.*

ATTERBURY, Marguerite Daisy, Ph.D. *Third generation American born missionary in Northern China. Former Welfare Commissioner for Chinese Intellectuals, Inc. Author and lecturer.*

CHAO, Tze-Chi, LL.D. *Senior Advisor to the ROC President. President of the World League for Freedom and Democracy.*

CHEN, Ellen M., Ph.D. *Professor of Chinese Philosophy, St. John's University.*

CHEN, Li-Fu, LL.D. *Former Minister of Education (1938-44), Professors of Chinese Culture, National Chen-Chi University and Chinese Culture University. Senior Advisor to the ROC President.*

CHEN, Samuel S. T., Ph.D. *Professor Emeritus of International Law and Organizations and history of Chinese Art, Central Connecticut State University. A prolific writer. For a list of his publications, see Victor T.H. Tsuan et al. (eds.) Selected Essays of Professor Samuel S. T. Chen (1991), p. 173.*

CHEN, Vincent, Ph.D. *Professor Emeritus of Political Science, St. John's University.*

CHENG, Stephen C. T., M.A. *is a singer and actor on Broadway and Television. Faculty of New York University, New School for Social Research, American Academy of Dramatic Arts and Stella Adler Consevatory of Acting.*

CHIEN, Fredrick, F. Ph.D. *Republic of China, Minister of Foreign Affairs.*

CHUNG, Charles C. M., M.A. *Former Adviser of the United Nations Secretariat. He is the author of "Question of Re-admitting the Republic of China to the United Nations" and other writings.*

ERSKINE, James Drummond, Lt. Col. *Vice President of the Manhattan Chapter of the U.S. Reserve Army Officers' Association. former Editor of the Guideposts International Edition. President, Shanghai Tiffin Club of New York, Inc.*

GARSIDE, Bettis A., L.H.D. *Former Professor of English, Chiloo University. Former Executive Director of the American Bureau for Medical Aid to China, Inc.*

HAU, Pei-Tsun, *Former Chief of General Staff, former Minister of National defense and Former ROC Premier. Senior Adviser to ROC President.*

HEINLEIN, David A., M.A. *is a scholar of Japanese history and a prize-winning New Jersey poet.*

HUCKABEE, Mike, Governor of the State of Arkansas. *Chairman of the United States League for Freedom and Democracy.*

HU, Jason C. Ph.D. *Director-General of the ROC Government Information Office.*

JOEI, Bernard T. K., Ph.D. *Former Ambassador to Ivory Coast. Senior Adviser to the Ministry of Foreign Affairs.*

JOSEPH, Michael, *Senior copy editor, The Free China Journal, Taipei, Taiwan.*

KAO, Chien-Fu, *Co-founder of the Linnan School of Painting. Former Professor of Art, National Sun Yat-Sen university and National Central University.*

KAO, Diana L., Ph.D. *Professor Emeritus of Asian Studies, a Chinese linguist, City College of New York.*

About the Authors

KUBEK, Anthony, Ph.D. *Professor Emeritus of Political Science, Troy State University. Curator of the General Claire Lee Chennault Memorial Library of Asian and American Affairs.*

KUHN, Irene Corbally, *Former Reporter, Founder of the Overseas Women's Club. A writer and Editor of the Gourmet magazine.*

KUO, Wei-Fan, Ph.D. *Chairman of the national Endowment for Culture and Arts. Minister of Education.*

MA, Jacob K. J., *Former Professor of Journalism, Chinese Culture University Former legislator representing overseas Chinese. General Manager, Editor-in-Chief and Vice Chairman of the Board of Directors, the World Journal.*

SINGLAUB, John Kirk, Major General, U.S. Army (Ret.). *Former Chief of Staff, the United Nations Command in Korea. Former Commander of the Joint Unconventional Warfare Task Force in Vietnam.*

SUNG, Betty Lee, Ph.D. *Professor Emeritus of Asian Studies, City College of New York. Author of "Mountain of Gold" and many other books.*

TSUAN, Victor T. H., Ph.D., F.R.S., *Professor Emeritus of International Studies, Fairleigh Dickinson University. Fellow, Royal Society of Great Britian and Ireland.*

VILLA-REAL, Luis A., *Brigadier General, Republic of the Philippines (Ret.)*

WHITTAKER, Robert E., *Master Mariner; a former sea Captain and U.S. Naval Reserve Officer, an award-winning independent film & video producer and script writer/ poet / author. President, COMPASS Books - video - films.*

WOO, Jae-Seung, Ph.D. *Secretary-General of the World League for Freedom and Democracy & Professor of International Law & Organizations, Chungang University, Seoul, Korea.*

******